SPANISH

Just for Business

Caroline Shipton and Jane Millar

Study Guide

Oxford University Press

GW00716599

Oxford University Press Walton Street Oxford OX2 6DP

Oxford New York Toronto
Delhi Bombay Calcutta Madras Karachi
Petaling Jaya Singapore Hong Kong Tokyo
Nairobi Dar es Salaam Cape Town
Melbourne Auckland

and associated companies in

Berlin Ibadan

Oxford is a trade mark of Oxford University Press

ISBN 0 19 912125 7

Illustrations by Patricia Moffett, Joan Corlass and Gecko Ltd.

Acknowledgements
The authors wish to acknowledge the help of Matthew Hunter, June
Jones, Mike Parsons, Francisco de la Sierra and Fernando Abasolo for
their contribution to the research that went into this publication. They
also wish to thank Alison Williams and Dawn Holdman for their help
with the tapescript, and finally one kind Spanish telephone operator
for her help with the recorded messages.

The authors
Caroline Shipton is Director of Merseyside Language Export Centre.
Jane Millar is Director of Managed Learning, Oxford.

Series editors
Jane Millar and Marilyn Farr.

Printed and bound in Great Britain by
Butler & Tanner Ltd, Frome and London

Contents

About the course

Welcome to **Spanish *Just for Business,*** a short, practical language course for the hard-pressed business learner. This course will not turn you into a fluent Spanish speaker overnight but it will equip you with some basic communication skills in Spanish, and above all it will demonstrate that you are making the effort to learn the language of the country you want to do business in! It is suitable for business people who need to learn a little Spanish for their work. You can do most of your learning from the cassettes alone. This is because one of the aims of the course is to train you to understand spoken Spanish on the telephone, in meetings and in other situations where you are not able to refer to the printed word. We therefore recommend that you listen to each Unit at least once before you refer to any of the printed material, apart from the *Pen and paper exercises,* in the Study guide.

You'll hear a series of conversations in Spanish, as you follow the progress of representatives of two British companies selling their products in Spain. English narrators guide you through step by step, explaining the language you hear and inviting you to join in the dialogues. The accompanying Study guide contains much useful back-up information, and we strongly recommend that you use it regularly to consolidate your learning.

To get the most out of your course we recommend that you tackle it in the following way:

1 Do your initial learning of each Unit somewhere where you can really concentrate. Car journeys, though ideal for reinforcement, are not really suitable for the learning of new material.

2 Listen to the cassette as often as you can, every day if possible. 'Little and often' is the key to successful language learning. Don't expect to master a Unit by listening to it once only. You will need to listen to it several times and to replay difficult sections as often as necessary. Use pause and replay buttons if you have them and remember to make a note of the number on your tape counter as you begin a new Unit.

3 Read through the notes provided in the Study guide after listening to each Unit. These notes are intended to provide you with a summary of the new language contained in each Unit and with a visual reinforcement of what you have learned from the cassettes.

The notes on each Unit have five sections:

1 Language for you to use

This is the language you will need to produce yourself and therefore you should concentrate on learning and practising the language in this section. Do not go on to the next Unit until you feel you have mastered these words and expressions. Try to get someone else to test you once you have learned them thoroughly.

2 Language for you to recognize

The language in this section is what you have heard other people use on the cassette and what you must therefore learn to recognize. Although at this stage you only need a 'passive' knowledge of this language, it is important not to neglect this section as you need to understand in order to respond effectively. You may also want to 'activate' this language later on, if, for example, you are receiving instead of making a telephone call.

3 Pen and Paper Exercises

Every now and then, if you are listening to the cassettes, you will come across the mention of a *Pen and paper exercise*. These are optional exercises which will improve your listening skills. They do not require you to write anything in Spanish; in fact, all you usually need to do is tick a box or draw a line as you listen to the relevant part of your cassette again. Do these exercises the first time you listen to the tape if you feel ready, but some are more difficult and you may need to come back to them later.

4 Language maps

These are a summary in diagrammatic or illustrated form of the dialogues you have heard on the cassettes complete with possible variations. They will help you make up and practise your own dialogues.

5 Language debrief

As well as a brief *Language reference section* at the back, we also guide you through some basic points about the structure of the language as they come up in each Unit.

At the end of the Guide you will find a *Language reference section*, a *Vocabulary section*, the answers to the *Pen and paper exercises* and some useful tips about doing business in Spain. We also suggest how you can develop your Spanish once you have completed this course.

Your pack also contains some prompt cards with key phrases for you to remember. You can slip them into your diary and use them for instant recall, when you are conversing in Spanish.

Unit 1 *Making contact by telephone*

By the end of this Unit you should be able to:

❏ get through to the right person

❏ deal with some difficulties

❏ understand when to call back.

But you'll have to wait till the next Unit to learn how
to leave a message yourself!

Key words and phrases
for you to use

Greetings and introductions

Hola	*Hello*
Buenos días	*Good morning (until 2 pm)*
Buenas tardes	*Good afternoon/evening (any time after 4 pm)*
Buenas noches	*Good night (only said as you go off to bed!)*
Adiós	*Goodbye*
Soy ...... de la compañía ...... de ...... , Inglaterra	*My name is ...... from .... Ltd, in ...... , in the UK*

Getting through to the right person

Quisiera hablar con el señor ...... /la señora	*I'd like to speak to Mr ...... /Mrs ......*
Quiero hablar con la señorita	*I want to speak to Miss ......*
¿Me pone con el señor ...... /la señora ...... , por favor?	*Can I speak to Mr ...... /Mrs ......, please?*
El señor ...... /La señora ...... , por favor	*Mr ...... /Mrs ...... , please*

Getting through to the right department

	El departamento de marketing, por favor	*Marketing department, please*

	técnico	*Technical*	
	de producción	*Production*	
	de importación	*Import*	
	de exportación	*Export*	
El departamento	de personal	*Personnel*	*Department*
	de contabilidad	*Accounts*	
	de compras	*Purchasing*	
	de ventas	*Sales*	
	de asistencia posventa	*After-sales service*	

Saying when you'll call back

No gracias, (le) llamaré ...	No thanks, I'll call (him/her) back ...
más tarde	later
esta tarde	this afternoon
mañana, por la mañana	tomorrow morning
mañana, por la tarde	tomorrow afternoon
la semana que viene	next week
el lunes	on Monday
el martes	on Tuesday
el miércoles	on Wednesday
el jueves	on Thursday
el viernes	on Friday
¿Cuándo puedo llamarle?	When can I call him/her (back)?

Other useful phrases

Buenos días, ¿habla Vd inglés?	Good morning, do you speak English?
¡Por supuesto!	Of course!
¡No, lo siento!	No, I'm sorry!
Sí, gracias	Yes, thanks
De acuerdo	O.K.
Muchas gracias	Thank you very much
Es decir	That is/ In other words
Perdone. No le entiendo bien	Excuse me. I don't understand (you)
¿Puede repetirlo (más despacio), por favor?	Could you repeat that (more slowly), please?

Key words and phrases
for you to recognize

Greetings you will hear

...... Buenos días. ¡Dígame!	...... *Good morning.* *Can I help you?*

Putting you through

¿De parte de quién?	*Who's speaking, please?*
Muy bien	*Very well*
No cuelgue, por favor	*Hold on, please*
Está comunicando	*The line's engaged*
Está hablando por teléfono ahora	*He/She is on the line at the moment*
¿Quiere esperar un momento?	*Would you like to hold?*
Ahora le paso/pongo	*I'm putting you through*
Oficina del señor Abasolo /de la señora Ortega	*Mr/Mrs ......'s office*
Julia Ortega al habla	*Julia Ortega on the line*

Sorry, I didn't catch that

¿Me puede repetir/deletrear su nombre, por favor?	*Could you repeat/spell your name, please?*
¿Cómo se escribe?	*How do you spell that?*

Understanding why they're not there

Lo siento	*I'm sorry*
No sé exactamente	*I'm not quite sure*
El señor ...... no está esta semana	*Mr ...... isn't here this week*
La señora ...... no está en este momento	*Mrs ...... isn't here at the moment*
La señorita ...... no está hoy	*Miss ...... isn't here today*
Está...	*He/She is ...*
fuera	*away*
en viaje de negocios	*away on business*
reunido/a	*in a meeting*
en reunión	*in a meeting*
de vacaciones	*on holiday*
enfermo/a	*ill*
ocupado/a	*busy*

And when you can call back

Puede llamarle ...	*You can call him/her (back) ...*
sobre las dos	*about 2 o'clock*
antes de las once	*before 11*
esta tarde	*this afternoon*
por la tarde	*in the afternoon*
mañana por la mañana	*tomorrow morning*
más tarde, esta mañana	*later, this morning*
pasado mañana	*the day after tomorrow*
la semana que viene	*next week*
el lunes que viene	*next Monday*

Section 3 **Pen and paper exercises**

The answers to all *Pen and paper exercises* can be found in the section beginning on p 79.

1 Listen to the tape and match the people to the departments in which they work.

    1 Technical services   a Sr Navarro
    2 After-sales service   b Sr Hernandez
    3 Marketing   c Srta Miguélez
    4 Accounts   d Sra Marañón

2 Write down the names of people and places as the caller spells them for you.

    1 _____

    2 _____

3 The pictures below show the *real* reasons why the person you are calling can't speak to you. Listen to the tape and tick the appropriate box to indicate whether the reason you hear is true or false.

  ☐ *True*   ☐ *False*   ☐ *True*   ☐ *False*

  ☐ *True*   ☐ *False*   ☐ *True*   ☐ *False*

4 Listen to Sra Serna and enter in your diary below the one time when you and Sr Cansino are both free to talk to each other on the phone.

Sunday

Monday — *TODAY*

11–12   Meeting with John Roberts, SCI TECH LTD

Tuesday

Wednesday

ALL-DAY SALES CONFERENCE
Dep. 7.30 a.m.
Home by 9pm?

Thursday

4.30pm. Dep. Heathrow – for Düsseldorf

Friday

TRADE FAIR – DÜSSELDORF
plane leaves 6.30p.m.

Saturday

Saying what you would like to do

Quisiera ...   *I'd like to ...*

To this phrase you can add the basic form of any verb (a word denoting an action) in order to say what you would like to do, e.g.

Quisiera hablar con el señor   *I'd like to talk to Mr Abasolo*
Abasolo

Quisiera llamar   *I'd like to call (back)*

Inviting someone to do something

¿Quiere ...?   *Would you like ...?*

Just as in the examples above, you can add verbs to this phrase if you want to invite someone to do something, e.g.

¿Quiere hablar con el   *Would you like to speak to*
señor Abasolo?   *Mr Abasolo?*

¿Quiere deletrear su   *Would you like to spell your*
 nombre?   *name?*

¿Quiere llamar?   *Would you like to ring back?*

Introducing yourself

When introducing themselves on the telephone or face-to-face Spanish people never say: Hello, it's *Mr* Smith or Hello, it's *Mrs* Jones. Instead, they always announce themselves by their full name, e.g.

Soy Fernando Abasolo ...   *It's Fernando Abasolo ...*

Soy Mari-Carmen López ...   *It's Mari-Carmen López ...*

Asking questions

Questions which require the answer 'yes' or 'no'

There are three common ways of asking this type of question in Spanish:

1 By letting your voice go up at the beginning of the sentence, e.g.

    ¿Quiere repetir su nombre? *Can you repeat your name?*

2 By changing the word order, e.g.

    ¿Habla Vd inglés?   *Do you speak English?*

3 By putting **verdad** or **no**, (which in this context mean nothing in themselves but merely indicate that a question is being asked) at the end, e.g.

    Vd habla inglés, **¿verdad?**   *Do you speak English?*
    or Vd habla inglés, **¿no?**

NB Questions are preceded as well as followed by question marks to let us know that a question is coming up! e.g.

    ¿Quiere repetir su nombre? *Can you repeat your name?*

Questions beginning with a question word

By this we mean questions beginning with words like *when, where, how, how much, why,* etc. Simply place the question word before the verb as in the question:

¿Cuándo puedo llamarle?   *When can I ring him (back)?*

We'll discuss other question forms as we meet them.

Language map

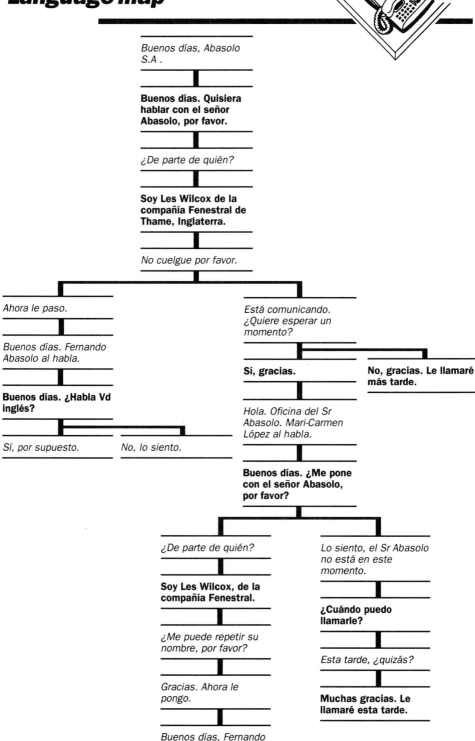

Buenos días, Abasolo S.A .

Buenos días. Quisiera hablar con el señor Abasolo, por favor.

¿De parte de quién?

Soy Les Wilcox de la compañía Fenestral de Thame, Inglaterra.

No cuelgue por favor.

Ahora le paso.

Buenos días. Fernando Abasolo al habla.

Buenos días. ¿Habla Vd inglés?

Sí, por supuesto.   No, lo siento.

Está comunicando. ¿Quiere esperar un momento?

Sí, gracias.   **No, gracias. Le llamaré más tarde.**

Hola. Oficina del Sr Abasolo. Mari-Carmen López al habla.

Buenos días. ¿Me pone con el señor Abasolo, por favor?

¿De parte de quién?

Soy Les Wilcox, de la compañía Fenestral.

¿Me puede repetir su nombre, por favor?

Gracias. Ahora le pongo.

Buenos días, Fernando Abasolo al habla.

Lo siento, el Sr Abasolo no está en este momento.

¿Cuándo puedo llamarle?

Esta tarde, ¿quizás?

Muchas gracias. Le llamaré esta tarde.

Unit 2 *More about telephoning*

By the end of this Unit you should be able to:

❏ deal confidently with telephone numbers
❏ leave basic details about yourself including
   what you are phoning about and
❏ ask for someone to ring you back.

You will also be able to make, change and cancel
appointments.

Key words and phrases
for you to use

Leaving basic details about who you are

El nombre de mi empresa es ...... *or* Mi empresa se llama	*The name of my company is ......*
La dirección de mi empresa es	*The address of my company is ......*
El número de teléfono es	*The telephone number is ......*
El prefijo es	*The code is ......*

Saying what you are telephoning for

Se trata de...	*It's about ...*
su carta	*your letter*
nuestro contrato	*our contract*
nuestra factura	*our invoice*
su visita a nuestra fábrica	*your visit to our factory*

Leaving a message for someone to ring back

¿Me puede llamar...	*Can he/she ring back...*
antes de las once y media?	*before 11.30?*
dentro de quince minutos?	*in 15 minutes?*
urgentemente?	*urgently?*

Talking about appointments

Requesting an appointment

Quisiera concertar una cita con ...	*I'd like to make an appointment with ...*

Fixing a date

La primera semana de septiembre, si es posible	*The first week of September, if possible*
Estoy libre el miércoles o el jueves	*I'm free on Wednesday or Thursday*

Changing a date

¿Podría cambiar/adelantar/aplazar la fecha de la reunión?	*Could you change/bring forward/postpone the date of the meeting?*

Confirming and cancelling appointments

Quisiera/Quiero confirmar/cancelar nuestra reunión del 18 de febrero	*I'd like to confirm/cancel our meeting of 18th February*

Useful phrases

Es urgente	*It's urgent*
No es necessario	*It's not necessary*

Key words and phrases
for you to recognize

Understanding requests for basic information

¿Cuál es su nombre? *or* ¿Cómo se llama Vd?	*What is your name?*
¿Cómo se llama su empresa/ compañía?	*What is your company's name?*
¿Cuál es la dirección de su empresa?	*What is your company's address?*
¿Cuál es su número de teléfono?	*What is your telephone number?*
¿Cuál es su extensión?	*What is your extension?*
¿De qué se trata, por favor?	*What is it about?*

Understanding questions about messages

¿Quiere dejar un mensaje?	*Do you want to leave a message?*
De acuerdo	*O.K. (i.e. I understand the message)*

Understanding offers of assistance

¿En qué puedo servirle yo?	*How can I help you?*

Understanding questions about appointments

¿Qué día le conviene?	*Which day suits you?*
¿Qué fecha le viene mejor?	*Which date do you prefer?*
Voy a buscar su agenda	*I'll go and get his/her diary*

¿Qué le parece las cuatro de la tarde?	*Does 4 pm suit you?*
sobre las cuatro	*around four o'clock*
a las cuatro	*at four o'clock*

Other useful phrases

¿Qué hora es en Inglaterra/ España?	*What time is it in England/ Spain?*

1 If the telephone number you hear does not match the one given below, write the one you've heard in the space provided.

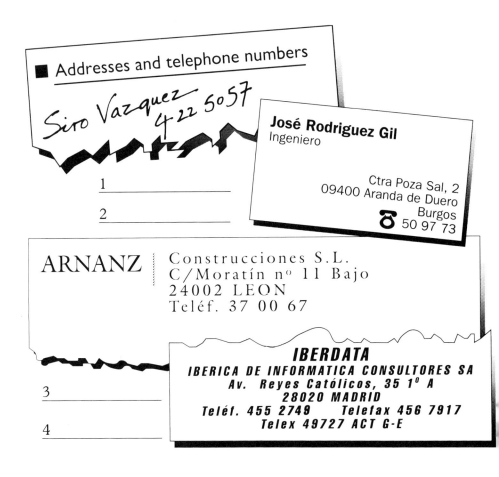

■ Addresses and telephone numbers

Siro Vazquez 4 22 5057

José Rodriguez Gil
Ingeniero

Ctra Poza Sal, 2
09400 Aranda de Duero
Burgos
☎ 50 97 73

1 _____

2 _____

ARNANZ Construcciones S.L.
C/Moratín nº 11 Bajo
24002 LEON
Teléf. 37 00 67

IBERDATA
IBERICA DE INFORMATICA CONSULTORES SA
Av. Reyes Católicos, 35 1º A
28020 MADRID
Teléf. 455 2749   Telefax 456 7917
Telex 49727 ACT G-E

3 _____

4 _____

2 Say the following telephone and fax numbers aloud after you hear the question on the tape. Then listen to the correct version.

1. 754 45 11   2. 72 03 19
3. 815 31 33   4. 67 18 77

3 Listen to the three conversations on tape and draw a line to link
   the message number firstly with the person or department it is for
   and then with the subject of the message. Take care! We've listed
   more people and messages than you actually hear!

Message 1   for   a) the Director's secretary   about   i)   a letter
Message 2   b) the Managing Director   ii) an invoice/bill
Message 3   c) Accounts   iii) a visit
                   d) Sales   iv) a contract

4 Listen to the answerphone messages and complete or amend the
   notes as necessary.

   1 Sr López from Samur called. He wants Mrs Phillips to ring
      him. I'm not sure what it's about, I'm afraid.

   2 Urgent message from Mariluz Cisneros of Forjados Rubiera
      for Mrs Cartwright, about something being cancelled. (Sorry,
      couldn't understand the rest!)

   3 Ana María Blanco from Ibelsa rang to confirm she'll be arriving
      at Heathrow on Thursday at 3 pm on flight BA264.

5 Number the recorded messages in the order in which you hear
   them.

                                                                   Number

   This subscriber has changed the first digit
   of his telephone number. Now it is a 5.

   The number you have just dialled is currently
   out of use.

   Because all the lines are busy, please dial
   again in a few minutes time.

Section 4 *Language debrief*

Masculine and feminine

In Spanish not just people, but all words denoting living beings, inanimate objects and concepts (nouns, grammatically speaking) have a gender, either masculine or feminine.

Other words which accompany nouns, such as the words for *the* and *a(n)*, or which replace them, such as *it* or *they*, must also take the appropriate masculine or feminine form; in grammatical terms, they must 'agree'.

Unfortunately there is no obvious logic to help one remember the gender of words. One simply has to learn them as one goes along. But don't worry about making mistakes in gender - you'll generally be understood even if you do.

'The' and 'a'

el/un señor	***the/a*** *gentleman*
la/una señora	***the/a*** *lady*

But this word is also masculine:

el/un departamento	***the/a*** *department*

whereas the word for 'section' is feminine:

la/una sección	***the/a*** *section*

There are also two words for the plural forms of *the,* namely **los** for masculine words e.g. **los** contratos ... *the contracts* and **las** for feminine words e.g. **las** facturas ... *the invoices.*

'Of the' (del/de la/de los/de las)

These forms all mean *of the*. The masculine **del** can be regarded as a contracted form of **de + el**. For example:

El jefe **del** departamento	*the head **of the** department*
de la sección	***of the** section*
de los dos departamentos	***of the** two departments*
de las tres empresas	***of the** three companies*

Asking 'what' and 'which'

To ask *What is ......* use **¿Cuál es?** e.g.

¿Cuál es su número de teléfono?   *What is your telephone number?*

In later units we'll meet:

¿Cuáles son ......?   *What are......?*

To ask *which ......* use **¿Qué......?** e.g.

¿Qué fecha le viene mejor?   *Which date suits you best?*

However, note that to ask *Which of the two ......* use **¿Cuál de los dos ......?** e.g.

¿Cuál de las fechas le viene mejor?   *Which of the dates suits you best?*

'Your' and 'our'

In the case of words meaning *your* there are different forms for singular and plural.

su nombre	*your name*
su dirección	*your address*
sus nombres	*your names*
sus facturas	*your invoices*

But for *our* there are different forms not only for singular and plural, but also for masculine and feminine! e.g.

nuestro número	*our number*
nuestra visita	*our visit*
nuestros contratos	*our contracts*
nuestras cartas	*our letters*

Saying what it's about

Se trata de nuestra visita	*It's about our visit*
¿De qué se trata?	*What is it about?*

Note that we say **¿De qué se trata?** literally *Of what is it about?* Remember that without this **de** the question is meaningless!

Asking whether it's possible

These are some more phrases to which you can add another verb, this time in order to ask if something is possible. They are all related in meaning, and come from the same verb, **poder** (*to be able*), about which you will find more information in the Language Reference section.

¿Puedo hablar con el Sr Martínez?	*Can I speak to Mr Martinez?*

Note this useful question that refers to both *you* and *he/she.*

¿Me puede llamar?	*Can **you***	
	*Can **he***	*call me back?*
	*Could **you***	
	*Could **he***	

Him and Her

In Unit 1, we learnt to say;

¿Puedo llamar**le** por la tarde?	*Can I ring **him/her** this afternoon?*

In Spanish **le** has a number of meanings, (*him, her, you, to him, to her, to you,*) and is positioned in a number of specific places in the utterance.

In the above example, we see it is tacked onto the end of the verb (because the verb is an infinitive). In Unit 2, we see it placed before the verb (because the verb is not an infinitive) as follows;

¿Qué día **le** conviene?	*Which day suits **you** (him/her)?*

Language map

Quisiera hablar con la Sra Ortega del departamento de compras.

Departamento de compras. Concha García al habla.

Buenos días. Soy Steve Hubert de la compañía Hubert Associates Ltd de Oxford, Inglaterra. Quistera hablar con la Sra. Ortega.

Lo siento, la señora Ortega está reunida ahora. ¿Quiere dejar un mensaje?

¿Me puede llamar esta tarde?

Sí por supuesto. ¿Me puede repetir su nombre por favor?

Soy Steve Hubert.

¿Y de qué empresa?

De Hubert Associates Ltd de Oxford, Inglaterra.

Gracias, y ¿qué es su número de telefono?

Es el 19-44 865 250903.

La señora Ortega está reunida esta tarde también. ¿En qué puedo servirle yo?

Quiero cambiar la fecha de nuestra cita del 8 de marzo.

¿Qué fecha le viene mejor?

El 9 de marzo, si es posible, a las cuatro de la tarde.

De acuerdo, señor Hubert. Adiós.

27

Unit 3 *Arriving at reception*

Checklist   By the end of this Unit you will be able to:

- ❏ announce yourself at reception
- ❏ say you have an appointment
- ❏ say what time your appointment is for
- ❏ introduce your companion(s)
- ❏ accept/refuse refreshments politely
- ❏ greet your host(ess)
- ❏ answer a few standard questions about your health, your journey and so on, with a few standard answers.

Key words and phrases
for you to use

At reception

Tengo / Tenemos una cita con el Sr/la Sra X	*I / We have an appointment with Mr/Mrs X*
Tengo una cita a las 10	*I have an appointment at 10 am*
¡Aquí tiene mi tarjeta!	*Here is my card!*
¡Un café, por favor!	*Coffee, please!*
...con leche y azúcar	*...with milk and sugar*
Prefiero té	*I prefer tea*
también	*also*

Meeting and greeting

¿Cómo está Vd? *or* ¿Qué tal está Vd?	*How are you?*
Muy bien gracias ¿y Vd?	*Very well thank you and you?*
¿Ha tenido Vd buen viaje?	*Did you have a good journey?*
Bien	*(it was) fine*
Regular	*(it was) not too bad*
Le presento al Sr Pérez	*May I introduce you to Mr Pérez*
... a mi compañero	*... to my colleague*
Encantado/a *or* Mucho gusto	*Pleased to meet you.*

Excuses, excuses

Lo siento	*I'm sorry/ I apologize*
La huelga!	*The strike!*
El retraso!	*The delay!*
El tráfico!	*The traffic!*
El embotellamiento!	*The traffic jam!*
Una caravana de 8 kilómetros!	*A 5 mile tail-back!*

Responding to apologies

No hay de qué	*It's not important*
No importa	*It doesn't matter*
No se preocupe, no tiene importancia	*Don't worry, it's all right/it doesn't matter*
Sí, perfectamente	*Yes, without difficulty/easily*
No, de ninguna manera	*No, not at all*

Key words and phrases
for you to recognize

At reception

¿Me dice su nombre por favor?	*Your name please?*
¿De parte de quién?	
¿Cómo?	*What did you say? (literally 'how')*
¿En qué puedo servirle?	*Can I help you?*
¿Qué desea?	
¿A qué hora tiene(n) Vd(s) la cita?	*What time is your appointment?*
¿Quiere(n) sentarse?	*Would you like to have a seat?*
¿Pueden esperar un poco/ unos minutos/un poco más?	*Can you wait for a while/a few minutes/a bit longer?*
Voy a avisar al Sr X que Vd(s) ha(n) llegado	*I'll let Mr X know that you have arrived*
Voy a buscar al Sr X	*I'll go and get Mr X*
El Sr X está reunido todavía	*Mr X is still in a meeting*
El Sr X todavía no ha vuelto de comer	*Mr X hasn't returned from lunch yet*
¿Desea(n) tomar algo ... café, té, o un refresco?	*Would you like a drink ... coffee, tea or a soft drink?*
¿Cómo lo quiere(n) ... solo, con leche o cortado?	*How would you like it ... black, with milk, or with only a dash of milk?*

NB Spanish people normally drink black coffee or coffee with very little milk, both in very small cups. Get used to asking for **un café con leche en taza grande** in order to get a large milky coffee.

Meeting and greeting

Siento haberle(s) hecho esperar	*I'm sorry for keeping you waiting*
¿Le(s) he hecho esperar?	*Have I kept you waiting?*
¿Ha(n) encontrado fácilmente la oficina?	*Did you find the office easily?*
Quiere(n) seguirme	*Please follow me*
Vamos a pasar a mi despacho	*Let's go through to my office*

Excuses, excuses

¡Una reunión muy larga!	*An endless meeting!*
¡Una comida muy prolongada!	*An endless lunch!*

1 Listen to the two receptionists talking about the visitors they expect, and complete the schedule. The visitors' names are listed below. Write the names in the appropriate spaces. Note that two visitors have an appointment at the same time.

Los visitantes: Isabel Pérez, Castilla Díaz SA
Rafael Giménez, CAF
Luis Velasco, auditoría interna
María Gutierrez, agencia de publicidad

Lunes   10 de Junio

Hora	Visitante	Para
10.30		Teresa Marañón dept de marketing
		Juan García dept. de compras
11.00		José Hernández servicio técnico
11.30		Alfonso Navarro contabilidad

2 Can you sort out this dialogue between June and the receptionist? Reorder the letters as appropriate. June speaks first.

a) *June*: Les Wilcox y June James de Fenestral.
b) *June*: A las once.
c) *Receptionist*: ¿De parte de quién, por favor?
d) *June*: Aquí tiene mi tarjeta.
e) *Receptionist*: ¿Quieren sentarse? Voy a avisar al Sr Abasolo.
f) *Receptionist*: ¿Cómo?
g) *June*: Buenos días. Tenemos una cita con el Sr Abasolo.
h) *Receptionist*: Gracias. ¿A qué hora tienen Vds la cita?

Language debrief

A look at verbs

English verbs generally have two present tense forms, whose use depends on who the doer is, e.g. *I speak,* but *she speaks, you work,* but *he works.*

It's rather like this in Spanish, except that almost every doer, *I, you, he, she, it, we* or *they,* has his, her or their own form of the verb.

The differences, which mostly involve changes in the way the word ends, can be very clearly heard and are easily identified.

Spanish verbs divide into several groups which each have typical forms. One of the biggest groups is those whose basic form (the form you find when you look in a dictionary) ends in **-ar**. Two verbs of this type which we have met so far are: **hablar** *(to speak),* and **llamar** *(to call back).*

Here are the different forms of these verbs for each person:

I	hablo	llamo
(Vd) he/she	habla	llama
(Vds) they	hablan	llaman
we	hablamos	llamamos

Listen out for the correct pronunciation in examples on the tape.

However the forms for the other persons follow different patterns. We've given you an example of each in the Language Reference section.

'Vd'

The Spanish are very polite in business and will refer to you as **Vd** (pronounced 'Usted'). This old form of address dates back to the 16th century and means *your honour.* The Spanish are never familiar with new acquaintances and use this form to show the correct respect and distance between people in a formal context.

This form is very easy to use as it takes the same form as *he* and *she* when referring to one person, e.g.

Vd puede llamar esta tarde   *You can ring back this afternoon*

¿Cuándo puede llamarme el Sr Martínez ?   *When can Mr Martínez ring me?*

When referring to more than one person it takes the same form as *they,* e.g.

¿Qué quieren tomar?   *What would you (or they) like to drink?*

Having and being able

Not a chapter from a philosophical treatise, but a note on two very common, but highly irregular verbs, **poder** *(to be able)* and **tener** *(to have)*. Because they are so common you will no doubt learn them quickly, despite their irregularity.

There are different forms of these verbs for each person (watch out for the oddities in spelling and practise with your tape to get the correct pronunciation).

I	puedo	tengo
he, she (Vd)	puede	tiene
they (Vds)	pueden	tienen
we	podemos	tenemos

Here are some of the contexts in which we have so far met these verbs.

poder: ¿**Puedo** llamarle?
¿Me **puede** repetir su nombre?

tener: **Tengo** una cita con el Sr Abasolo
Tenemos una cita con la Sra Ortega
Tiene una cita con el Sr Navarro

Handing something over

As you give an object to someone, you say in Spanish:

Aquí tiene mi tarjeta *Here's my card*

Aquí tiene nuestro folleto *Here's my brochure*

Being negative

Not an attitude we would wish to encourage, but sometimes it's necessary. To say *not,* use **no...** as in:

No importa, **no** tiene importancia *Don't worry, it's alright. It's not important*

No tenemos té *We haven't any tea*

You'll find some more examples in the recording for Unit 4. Note that in Spanish, when we say:

No, no tiene importancia *No, it's not important*

No is repeated twice.

Language map

Sí, señor?

Buenos días. Tenemos una cita con el Sr Abasolo.

¿De parte de quién?

El Sr Wilcox y la Sra James de la empresa Fenestral.

¿A qué hora tienen Vds la cita?

Tenemos la cita a las once.

Quieren sentarse. Voy a avisar al Sr Abasolo.

El señor Abasolo llega a recepción

Sr Wilcox, ¿cómo está Vd?

Muy bien, gracias.

¿Han tenido Vds un buen viaje?

Regular, gracias.

Le presento a mi socio, la Sra James.

Encantado. Quieren seguirme. Vamos a pasar a mi despacho.

Lo siento pero el Sr Abasolo está todavía reunido ...¿Quieren tomar algo?... ¿un café, té o un refresco?

Sí, dos cafés, por favor.

¿Cómo lo quieren ... solo, con leche o cortado?

Con leche, por favor.

¿Quieren azúcar?

No, gracias.

Sr Wilcox, siento haberles hecho esperar.

No se preocupe, no tiene importancia.

Unit 4 *Presenting your company and its products I*

Checklist   By the end of this Unit, you will have learnt:

❏ how to present yourself, your company and your products

❏ how to talk about dimensions

❏ how to talk about delivery terms and payment.

You will also learn a few basic strategies for meetings and to ask intelligent questions in Spanish as you go round the Spanish company.

Key words and phrases
for you to use

Introducing yourself and others

Soy/Le presento a ...	*I am/Let me introduce ...*
el director/la directora del departamento de exportación	*the export director*
Perdone, no le he entendido	*Excuse me, I haven't understood (you)*

NB In Spain, it is considered impolite to say bluntly 'I haven't understood.' It is acceptable, however, to say 'I haven't understood *you*.'

Presenting the company

Somos una empresa mediana	*We are a medium-sized company*
La empresa se fundó hace cuarenta años	*The company was founded 40 years ago*
Fabricamos ventanas	*We make windows*
ventanas/jerseys hechos a mano/x ventanas/ jerseys por mes	*windows/hand-made jumpers /x windows/ jumpers a month*
Queremos introducirnos en el mercado español	*We want to export to Spain*
Actualmente ...	*At the moment ...*
... actualmente	*... right now/at this very moment*

NB **actualmente** never means *actually*

Estamos especializados en ...	*We specialize in ...*
Tenemos ...	*We have ...*
aproximadamente cien empleados	*about 100 employees*
x unidades de producción	*x production units*
una gama amplia de productos	*a large product range*

x por ciento del mercado interior/ holandés	*x% of the home/ Dutch market*
Tenemos en proyecto el lanzamiento de un nuevo producto	*We intend to launch a new product*
Nuestro volumen de ventas es seiscientos millones de pesetas	*Our turnover is 600 millon pesetas*

Presenting the product

Its quality

Es un producto	*It's a ......*
de alta calidad	*high quality*
fuerte	*strong*
moderno	*modern*
práctico	*practical product*

Its dimensions

Nuestro producto tiene 250 centímetros/milímetros	*Our product is 250 cm/mm. ......*
de largo	*long*
de ancho	*wide*
de alto	*tall*
de diámetro	*in diameter*
de espesor	*thick*

What it's made of

Nuestro producto es	*Our product is in/made of ......*
de aluminio	*aluminium*
de madera	*wood*
de cartón	*cardboard*
de uPVC	*uPVC*
de cristal	*glass*

Price and delivery

Fabricamos sobre pedido	*We make to order*
Aquí tiene una lista de precios	*Here is a price list*
Tenemos unos precios muy competitivos	*We have attractive prices*
Hay un descuento de x por ciento	*There is a discount of x%*
¿Cuál es el plazo de la entrega?	*How long do deliveries take?*
Un mes y medio/seis semanas	*A month and a half/six weeks*
Preferimos el crédito documentario irrevocable	*We prefer (payment by) irrevocable letter of credit*
Fabricamos varios modelos de serie	*We make several standard styles*

Tactical phrases for meetings

¡Es una pregunta muy interesante!	*That's a very interesting question!*
Me informaré	*I'll find out*
Lo comprobaré en la oficina	*I'll check with the office*
Lo hemos comprobado	*We've checked*
Perdone, creo que hay una pequeña confusión	*Sorry! I think there's been a slight misunderstanding.*
Si le he entendido bien, quiere hacer un pedido	*If I've understood correctly, you want to place an order*

Asking business-related questions

¿Fabrican (Vds) sus propias piezas?	*Do you make your own parts?*
¿Tienen (Vds) transporte propio?	*Do you have your own lorries?*
¿Quiénes son sus clientes?	*Who are your clients?*
¿Trabajan (Vds) con compañías grandes?	*Do you work with big companies?*
¿Compran (Vds) las piezas en la provincia?	*Do you buy your parts locally?*
¿Cuántos proveedores tienen (Vds)?	*How many suppliers do you use?*

Useful expressions

¡Es cierto!	*It's true!/That's true!*
¡Depende!	*It depends!*

Key words and phrases
for you to recognize

Understanding questions about your company

¿Cuál es su volumen de ventas?	*What is your turnover?*
¿Cuál es su participación en el mercado español?	*What share of the Spanish market do you have?*
¿Cuántas fábricas tienen (Vds)?	*How many factories do you have?*
¿Cuántas ventanas/jerseys fabrican (Vds) por semana/mes?	*How many windows/pullovers do you make per week/month?*
¿Tienen (Vds) una gama amplia de productos?	*Do you have a large product range?*

Understanding questions about your products

¿Cuáles son las dimensiones de su producto?	*What are the dimensions of your product?*
¿Fabrican (Vds) muchos modelos/tamaños?	*Do you manufacture lots of models/sizes?*
¿De qué material son sus productos?	*What are your products made of?*
¿Cumplen sus productos las nuevas normas europeas?	*Do your products conform to the new European standards?*
¿Venden (Vds) piezas de recambio/piezas de repuesto?	*Do you supply (spare) parts?*

Understanding questions about delivery terms and payment

¿Tienen (Vds) muchas ventanas en stock?	*Do you have lots of windows in stock?*
¿Fabrican (Vds) sobre pedido?	*Do you manufacture to order?*
¿Tienen (Vds) una lista de precios?	*Do you have a price list?*
¿Hacen (Vds) descuento?	*Do you give discounts?*
¿Cuál es el plazo de entrega?	*How long do deliveries take?*
¿Cuáles son sus condiciones de pago?	*What are your terms of payment?*
¿Me puede dar el precio en pesetas?	*Can you give me the price in pesetas?*

Understanding your guide on the tour of the premises

Aquí está la cadena de producción	*Here you have the production line*
A la derecha/izquierda está el almacén/la zona de embalaje	*To the right/to the left we have the storage/packing area*
¿Qué clase de embalaje utilizan (Vds)?	*What you use as packaging?*
Voy a enseñarle	*I'll show you*

A useful phrase to recognize

¡No me extraña!	*I'm not surprised!/I might have guessed!*

47

1 Listen to June enumerating the benefits of Fenestral's windows and number the statements reprinted below in the order in which you hear them.

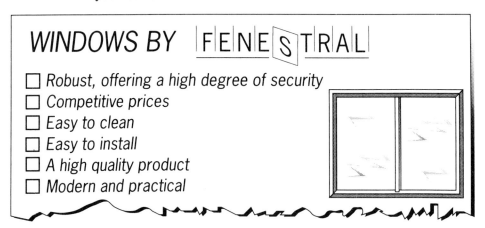

WINDOWS BY |F|E|N|E|S|T|R|A|L|

☐ *Robust, offering a high degree of security*
☐ *Competitive prices*
☐ *Easy to clean*
☐ *Easy to install*
☐ *A high quality product*
☐ *Modern and practical*

2 Listen to the conversations and fill in the dimensions.

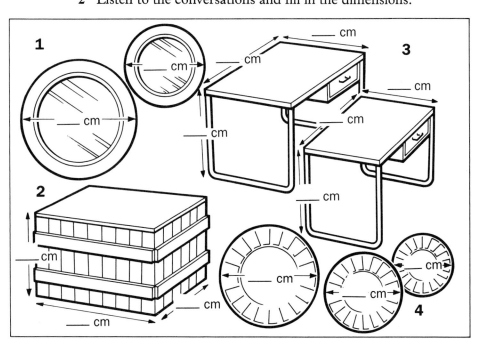

Presenting your company

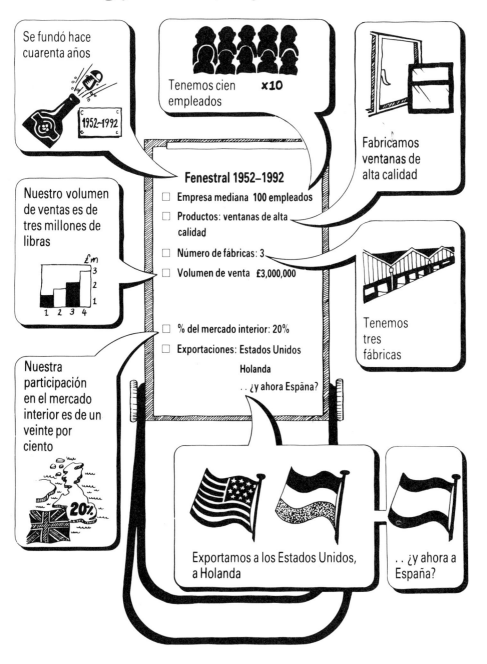

Se fundó hace cuarenta años

1952–1992

Tenemos cien empleados **x10**

Fabricamos ventanas de alta calidad

Nuestro volumen de ventas es de tres millones de libras

Fenestral 1952–1992

☐ Empresa mediana 100 empleados
☐ Productos: ventanas de alta calidad
☐ Número de fábricas: 3
☐ Volumen de venta £3,000,000

☐ % del mercado interior: 20%
☐ Exportaciones: Estados Unidos
   Holanda
   .. ¿y ahora Espāna?

Tenemos tres fábricas

Nuestra participación en el mercado interior es de un veinte por ciento

20%

Exportamos a los Estados Unidos, a Holanda

.. ¿y ahora a España?

Presenting your product

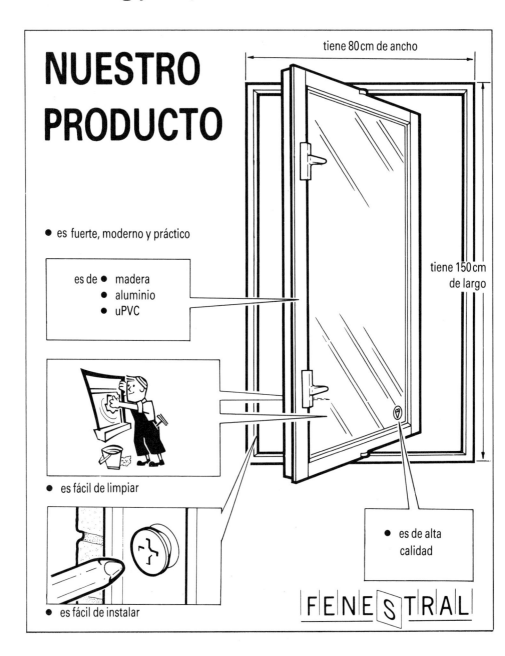

NUESTRO PRODUCTO

tiene 80 cm de ancho

tiene 150 cm de largo

- es fuerte, moderno y práctico

es de
- madera
- aluminio
- uPVC

- es fácil de limpiar

- es fácil de instalar

- es de alta calidad

FENESTRAL

Fixing the terms

¿Hacen Vds descuento?

¿Cuál es el plazo de entrega?

¿Tienen Vds una lista de precios?

¿Cuáles son las condiciones de pago?

Sí, el quince por ciento

Seis semanas

Aquí tiene una lista de precios

Preferimos el crédito documentario irrevocable

'Since' and 'ago'

The company was established forty years *ago*; June tells Sr Abasolo:

La empresa se fundó *hace* 40 años.

Later, in Unit 6, Les will say that he has been working for Fenestral *for* a long time:

Trabajo para Fenestral *desde hace* mucho tiempo.

He could have said he has been working for Fenestral *for* 4 years, *desde hace* **4 años,** or *since 1985,* **desde 1985.**

Asking how many

¿**Cuánto** ...? for singular	*How many ...*
¿**Cuántos** ...? for masculine plural	*How many ...*
¿**Cuántas...**? for feminine plural	*How many...*
¿Cuántas ventanas fabrican (Vds) por semana?	*How many windows do you make each week?*
¿ Cuántos empleados tienen (Vds)?	*How many workers do you have?*

In both these cases the question is asked using the reversed word order **fabrican Vds, tienen Vds.** However, note that the question is just as easily understood by omitting the **Vds,** and just as commonly heard.

¿Cuántas ventanas fabrican por semana? and
¿Cuántos empleados tienen?

The insertion or omission of the **Vd(s)** is not governed by grammatical rules and is more a matter of individual choice. You will hear each used as often as the other.

Masculine and feminine objects

As you know, even inanimate objects like windows (**la ventana**: feminine) have a gender in Spanish and so words to describe them must also be given a gender.

Certain words such as **fuerte** do not change but those which end in **o** such as **moderno** and **práctico** must change when used to describe objects which are feminine e.g.

La ventan**a** es **fuerte**, modern**a** y práctic**a**	*The window is robust, modern and practical*
El porcentaje exact**o** es 25%	*The exact percentage is 25%*

So far the examples given have been in the singular, but the changes must also be made when the words are used in the plural e.g.

Las vent**as** en Holanda están consolidad**as**	*Sales in Holland are very good*

and

Tenemos un**os** preci**os** muy competitiv**os**	*We have very competitive prices*
Las ventan**as** son fuerte**s**	*The windows are robust*

These examples show that all words used to describe the noun need to agree with it e.g.

Las nuev**as** norm**as** europe**as** (all feminine)	*The new European standards*
Preferimos **el** crédit**o** documentari**o** irrevocable (all masculine)	*We prefer irrevocable documentary credit*

Talking about dimensions

There is a standard pattern you can use to express the dimensions of an object, as follows:

Tiene ...... cm ...	*It's ...... cm ...*
de largo	*long*
de ancho	*wide*
de alto	*high/tall*

| de diámetro | *in diameter* |
| de espesor | *thick* |

Describing people and objects

When in English we use a word to describe a person or an object (in grammatical terms, an adjective), we place it before that person or thing, e.g. a robust model, a typical window. In Spanish (as a general rule) you must place the adjective after the word it describes, e.g.

| una ventana **típica** | *a **typical** window* |
| un modelo **fuerte** | *a **robust** model* |

Some adjectives change their meaning when placed before the word it describes, e.g. **nuevo/a**

| una **nueva** norma | *a brand new standard* |
| una norma **nueva** | *a fresh/another standard* |

grande not only changes its meaning when placed before a noun, it also loses the final '-de'.

| un hombre **grande** | *a tall man* |
| un **gran** hombre | *a great (important) man* |

Other adjectives also lose the last syllable, e.g. **primero** *first* becomes **primer** as in the phrase **como primer plato** *as a first course* (see Unit 6).

Remember that you can often omit the noun when you go on to compare different features of the same object, e.g.

la ventana grande y la ventana pequeña or
la grande y la pequeña

Unit 5 *Presenting your company and its products II*

Checklist In this Unit you will learn more about:

❏ presenting yourself, your company and your product.

You will also learn:

❏ how to ask and answer questions about the market
❏ how to talk in percentages.

Key words and phrases
for you to use

Introducing yourself

Soy el director/la directora de *I am the director of a small family*
una pequeña empresa familiar *business*

Talking about your workforce

Tenemos equipos de   *We employ teams of specialised*
empleados especializados a *home-based workers*
domicilio

Talking about your products

La calidad de nuestros   *The quality of our products is*
productos está garantizada *guaranteed*

Talking about your company's performance

Este año, nuestras ventas han *Our sales this year have increased*
aumentado en un cincuenta   *by 50% compared to last year*
por ciento con relación al año
anterior

Nuestras ventas en los   *We are selling very well in the*
Estados Unidos/en Japón/en *States/in Japan/in Germany*
Alemania están consolidadas

Talking about your customers

Los españoles, como los   *The Spanish, like the Americans,*
americanos, aprecian la   *appreciate quality*
calidad

Researching the market for your product

¿Cuántos jerseys escoceses venden (Vds) ...	*How many Scottish pullovers do you sell ...*
por semana?	*per week?*
por mes?	*per month?*
por año?	*per year?*
¿Cuál es su tipo de clientela?	*Who is your typical client?*
¿Qué tallas se venden bien?	*Which sizes sell well?*
¿Están nuestros modelos bien adaptados al mercado español?	*Are our models well suited to the Spanish market?*

Talking about delivery terms and payment

Hacemos el envío por correo certificado	*We deliver by registered post*
Se paga contra factura	*You pay against invoice*

Taking your leave

Aquí tiene mi tarjeta/nuestro folleto/unos modelos	*Here is my card/our brochure/some samples*

Note There are two words for samples; for clothing it is more usual to say **modelo,** whereas for industrial products, samples are **muestras.**

Muchas gracias por su visita	*Thank you for your visit*
De nada. El gusto ha sido mío	*Think nothing of it. The pleasure was mine*

Useful expressions

¡Eso es/Es cierto/ Exactamente!	*That's right!*
¿Por qué no?	*Why not?*
¡He tomado nota!	*I've taken note*

Key words and phrases
for you to recognize

Understanding the hype

Hemos tenido mucho éxito con nuestros productos en todos los países europeos	*We are doing very well with our products in all European countries*
Ahora somos una compañía industrial de dimensión internacional con nuestra sede social en Bruselas	*We are now a company operating on an international scale with headquarters at Brussels*
Nuestro volumen de ventas del año pasado superó los doce billones de pesetas	*Our turnover last year exceeded 12 billion pesetas*
Tenemos x sucursales en el extranjero	*We have x branches abroad*
Nuestro crecimiento ha sido muy rápido	*Our growth has been very rapid*
No hay mucha competencia	*We haven't got much competition*
Tenemos el 25% del mercado interior	*We have 25% of the home market*

Understanding what the buyer says

En invierno se vende mejor que en verano	*In winter we sell better than in summer*
¿Cuál es nuestro tipo de clientela?	*Our typical client?*
Es el de una madre de familia que compra un jersey para su hija	*It would be a mother buying her daughter a pullover*
¿Qué tallas se venden bien? El treinta y ocho y el cuarenta	*Which sizes sell well? 38 and 40*

About your products

Me gustan mucho sus productos	*I like your products very much*
Son muy originales y ligeros ... (pero) los colores no son suficientemente vivos	*They're very original and lightweight ... (but) the colours are not bright enough*

Queries and requests from the buyer

¿Me puede dejar unos modelos?	*Can you leave me some samples?*
¿Cuál es el precio de una pieza suelta?	*What is the price of one single part?*
¿Tienen (Vds) todas las piezas en stock?	*Do you have all the parts in stock?*
¿Me puede confirmar el precio por carta?	*Will you confirm the quote by letter?*

Section 3 **Pen and paper exercises**

1 Listen to the interviews and complete the company profiles.

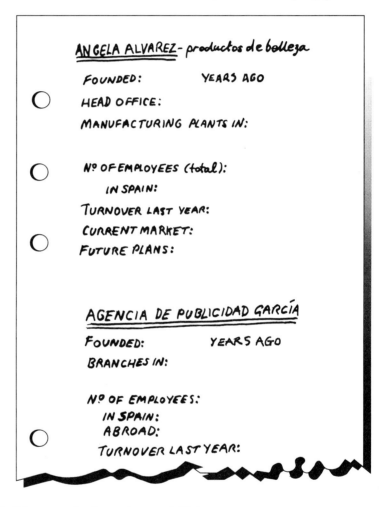

ANGELA ALVAREZ- *productos de belleza*

○ FOUNDED: YEARS AGO
    HEAD OFFICE:
    MANUFACTURING PLANTS IN:

○ Nº OF EMPLOYEES (total):
       IN SPAIN:
    TURNOVER LAST YEAR:
    CURRENT MARKET:
○ FUTURE PLANS:

AGENCIA DE PUBLICIDAD GARCÍA

    FOUNDED: YEARS AGO
    BRANCHES IN:

    Nº OF EMPLOYEES:
       IN SPAIN:
       ABROAD:
○ TURNOVER LAST YEAR:

2 Listen to the interview and fill in
the percentage represented by
each segment.

**Proportion of
turnover in
various markets**

Europe ___ %

Italy ___%

USA ___ %

The shaded areas represent the rate of increase in each market. Insert the figures.

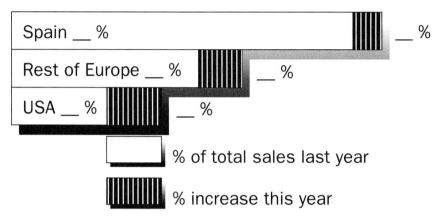

Spain __ %   __ %

Rest of Europe __ %   __ %

USA __ %   __ %

_____ % of total sales last year

% increase this year

3 Listen to the conversation and complete the notes.

	AX45	AX32
In stock?		
Delivery dates?		
Price?		
Do they give discounts?		
%?		
Method of payment?		

New markets

Tenemos una gama
amplia de productos . . .

Este año, nuestras ventas
han aumentado en un
cien por ciento . . .

Nuestras ventas en
Inglaterra, en Italia y en
Alemania están consolidadas . . .

Y ahora queremos
exportar a Japón.

Language map 2

Researching the market

¿Cuántos jerseys venden Vds por mes?

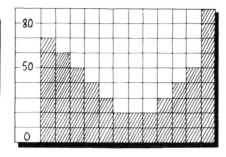

Depende. 50 o 60 de promedio. En invierno por supuesto, se vende mejor que en verano.

¿Cuál es su tipo de clientela?

Es el de una madre de familia que compra un jersey a su hija de veinte a treinta años.

¿Qué tallas se venden bien?

36	
38	✓
40	✓
42	
44	
48	

La treinta y ocho y la cuarenta, sobre todo.

¿Están sus modelos bien adaptados al mercado español?

	COLOR	PRECIO	MODELO
BIEN		✓	✓
BASTANTE BIEN			
MAL	✓		

Sí, pero los colores no son suficientemente vivos

63

Goods that sell themselves

If only they did! Unfortunately it happens only in a grammatical sense. Angela Alvarez said:

Nuestros productos **se** venden muy bien en España	literally: *Our products sell **themselves** very well in Spain*

However, if you talk about a person or a company selling goods, the word **se** disappears, e.g.

Nuestro concesionario/ Nuestra compañía vende muchos productos en España	*Our agent/ our company sells many goods in Spain*

Talking percentages

To express a percentage in Spanish is very straightforward:

Cinco por ciento	*5%*
Veinte por ciento	*20%*

Our various speakers talk about percentages in several contexts. Firstly in saying what percentage of a particular market they have:

Nuestra participación en el mercado interior es de un 20%	*We have 20% of the home market*

Secondly, in saying what percentage of production is sold where:

Vendemos el 53% de nuestra producción en el mercado interior	*We sell 53% of our production in the home market*

In talking about percentage increase of sales:

Nuestras ventas han aumentado en un 30% con relación al año anterior	*Our sales have increased 30% in comparison with last year*

And finally with reference to discounts:

Hay un descuento de 5%	*There's a discount of 5%*

Making comparisons

Steve refers to the discounts available on an order for more than 10 sweaters - **un pedido de más de diez jerseys**

más de	*more than*
menos de	*less than*

These are the phrases to use when you are comparing numbers or amounts of money. In other comparisons use **más que, menos que, mejor que,** etc, e.g.

Vendemos más que la competencia	*We sell more than our competitors*
En invierno, se vende mejor que en verano	*In winter, we sell better than in summer*

Asking about price

There are various ways of asking how much something costs. Either ask:

¿Cuál es el precio de ......?	*What is the price of ......?*
¿Cuánto cuesta/ vale ......?	*How much does this cost?*
¿Cuánto es?	*How much is it?*

Unit 6 *Eating out with business contacts*

Checklist   In this Unit you will learn to:

❑ order food and drink in a restaurant

❑ ask what things are, what is recommended and what is available

❑ say what you like and dislike.

You will also learn some small talk for the dinner table.

Key words and phrases
for you to use

Asking for help or information

¿Un fino? ¿ Eso qué es?	*A 'fino' ? What's that?*
¿Qué quesos/vinos/ postres tiene (Vd)?	*What do you have in the way of cheese/wine/dessert?*
¿Tiene (Vd) vinos del país?	*Do you have any local wines?*
¿Qué es lo que me puede recomendar?	*What do you recommend?*

Ordering

Quiero tomar un jamón de Jabugo	*I'll have a 'Jabugo' ham*
Quiero tomar un churrasco en su punto	*I'll have a medium steak*
La cuenta, por favor	*The bill, please*
¿Cuánto es?	*How much is that?*

Accepting/refusing

Sí, por supuesto/ Sí, gracias	*Yes, please!*
Sí, como no	*I wouldn't mind!*
Quiero probar el marisco	*I wouldn't mind trying the seafood*
¡No diré que no!	*I won't say no!*
¡Vd es muy amable!	*It's very kind of you!*
Gracias, no. He comido bien	*No thanks. I've had plenty.*
No, para mí, no. Gracias	*Not for me, thanks*
¡No hay de qué!	*Don't mention it!*

Expressing likes and dislikes

Me gusta mucho la cocina española	*I like Spanish cooking a lot*
No me gusta el marisco	*I don't like seafood*
Prefiero tomar agua mineral con gas	*I prefer fizzy mineral water*
Me encantan las patatas fritas/los pasteles	*I love chips/cakes*

Business talk

Mañana, me voy a Nueva York	*Tomorrow I'm going to New York*
Tengo una cita con ...	*I have an appointment with...*
Vuelvo a Inglaterra	*I'm going back to England*

Small talk

Estoy casado/a	*I'm married*
No estoy casado/a	*I'm not married*
Tengo dos hijos	*I have two children*
No tengo hijos	*I have no children*
Soy de Sheffield/Glasgow	*I'm from Sheffield/Glasgow*
Vivo en Londres/ Manchester	*I live in London/Manchester*
Fumo/No fumo	*I smoke/I do not smoke*
Trabajo para Fenestral desde hace x años	*I've been working at Fenestral for x years*
Viajo mucho	*I travel a lot*
Hace bueno/calor/frío	*It's fine/hot/cold*
Llueve/Nieva	*It's raining/It's snowing*

Key words and phrases
for you to recognize

Table talk

¿Quiere (Vd) cenar con nosotros esta noche?	*Would you like to have dinner with us?*
Voy a buscarle enseguida/ dentro de poco/a las nueve	*I'll come and pick you up straight away/in a little while/at 9 o'clock★*

Ordering food and drink

¿Quiere(n) Vd(s) tomar algo?	*Would you like something to drink?*
¿Quiere(n) Vd(s) tomar un aperitivo?	*Will you have an apéritif?*
¿Se lo pongo en la cuenta?	*Shall I put it on the bill?*
¿Esta mesa le(s) conviene?	*Is this table all right?*
¿Van a tomar el menú del día o van a pedir a la carta?	*Would you like the (fixed) menu or the à la carte menu?*
¿Quiere(n) probar una especialidad de la casa?	*Would you like to try a speciality of the house?*
¿Le gusta el jamón de Jabugo?	*Do you like cured ham?*
Le puedo sugerir el pescado	*I recommend the fish*
Le puedo recomendar la carne	*I suggest you try the meat*
Es un plato/vino típico de la provincia	*It's a typical dish/wine of the region*
¿Qué les puedo servir?	*(said by the waiter) 'Are you ready to order?'*
¿Para empezar...?	*To start with?*

★Dinner is eaten much later in Spain than in England. It is quite normal to arrive at the restaurant between 9 o'clock and midnight!

¿Y el plato principal/ postre?	*As a main course?/dessert?*
¿Prefiere Vd el churrasco en su punto o poco hecho?	*Do you prefer the steak medium or rare?*
¡Que aproveche!	*Have a good meal!*

Business talk

¿Los negocios van bien?	*Is business going well?*
¿Desde cuándo trabaja Vd para ...... ?	*How long have you been working for ...... ?*
¿Está(n) Vd(s) satisfecho(s)/ a(s) de su visita?	*Are you pleased with your visit to us?*
Vds vuelven a Inglaterra mañana, ¿no?	*You're going back to England tomorrow, aren't you?*

Small talk

General

¿Conoce Vd España/ la provincia de Madrid?	*Do you know Spain?/the province of Madrid?*
¿Es su primera visita a Madrid?	*Is it your first visit to Madrid?*
¿De dónde es Vd?	*Where are you from?*
¿Dónde vive Vd?	*Where do you live?*
¿Le molesta si fumo?	*Do you mind if I smoke?*
¿Es cierto que siempre llueve en Inglaterra?	*Is it true that it rains all the time in England?*
¿Es cierto que los ingleses comen el postre antes del queso?	*Is it true that the English eat dessert before cheese?*

Personal

Si me permite ...	*If I may be so bold ...*
¿está Vd casado/a?	*are you married?*
¿tiene Vd hijos?	*have you got any children?*
¿cuál es su nombre de pila?	*what's your first name?*

1 Listen to the conversation in the restaurant and tick those items on the menu which you hear mentioned.

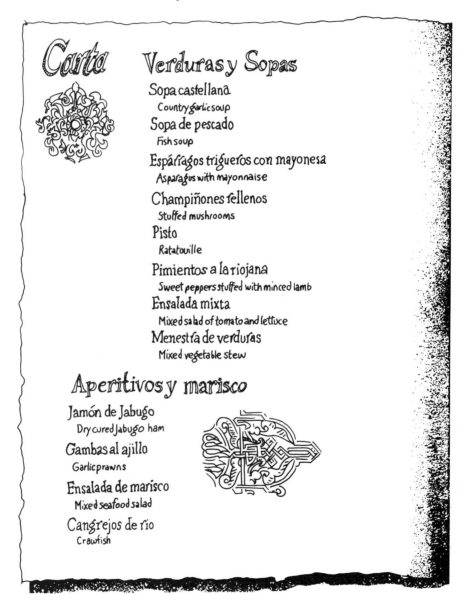

Carta

Verduras y Sopas

Sopa castellana
Country garlic soup

Sopa de pescado
Fish soup

Espárragos trigueros con mayonesa
Asparagus with mayonnaise

Champiñones rellenos
Stuffed mushrooms

Pisto
Ratatouille

Pimientos a la riojana
Sweet peppers stuffed with minced lamb

Ensalada mixta
Mixed salad of tomato and lettuce

Menestra de verduras
Mixed vegetable stew

Aperitivos y marisco

Jamón de Jabugo
Dry cured Jabugo ham

Gambas al ajillo
Garlic prawns

Ensalada de marisco
Mixed seafood salad

Cangrejos de río
Crawfish

Platos Principales

Carnes

Churrasco de ternera
  T-bone steak
Entrecote de buey
  Rib of beef
Cordero asado
  Roast lamb
Cochinillo asado
  Roast suckling pig
Riñones al jerez
  Kidneys braised in sherry

Avez y caza

Codornices estofadas
  Braised quail
Conejo al ajillo
  Braised rabbit with garlic
1/2 pollo asado
  Roast half chicken

Pescado

Besugo al horno
  Sea bream baked in the oven
Emperador a la plancha
  Grilled swordfish
Bonito con Tomate
  Tuna braised in tomato
Chipirones rebozadas
  Baby squid in batter

Calamares a la romana
  Battered squid rings
Merluza a la vasca
  Hake with green sauce made with parsley
  peas and garlic

2 Listen to the conversations between Mari-Carmen López and Les, and between June and Fernando Abasolo and then answer the questions.

1 How old are Les's children?

2 What is his wife's job? Does she work for Fenestral?

3 How long has Les been working for Fenestral?

4 Where does June live?

5 Does she have any children?

Asking what something is

Menus in other countries are full of unfamiliar things, so if you are going to sample fully the local cuisine, it's important to be able to ask what something is. The question you need in Spanish is:

¿Eso qué es?   *What is it?*

Asking what is available

¿Qué **vinos /coche** tiene Vd?
literally: *What **wines/car** do you have?*

This is a useful expression if you want to find out what is available within a particular category.

Isn't that right?

You may remember Julia Ortega's husband Jorge says:

Mi mujer es de Burgos,   *My wife is from Burgos, isn't*
¿verdad, querida?   *that right, darling?*

¿verdad? is a very useful phrase meaning *isn't that right?* It serves the same purpose as all those little questions like ...... *isn't it?*, ... *don't you?*, ... *shouldn't we?*, and so on, which we tag onto statements in English.

So if you were visibly enjoying your **ensalada de marisco** or **jamón de Jabugo,** your Spanish host might say:

Le gusta la cocina española,   *You like Spanish cooking, don't*
¿verdad?   *you?*

Language map

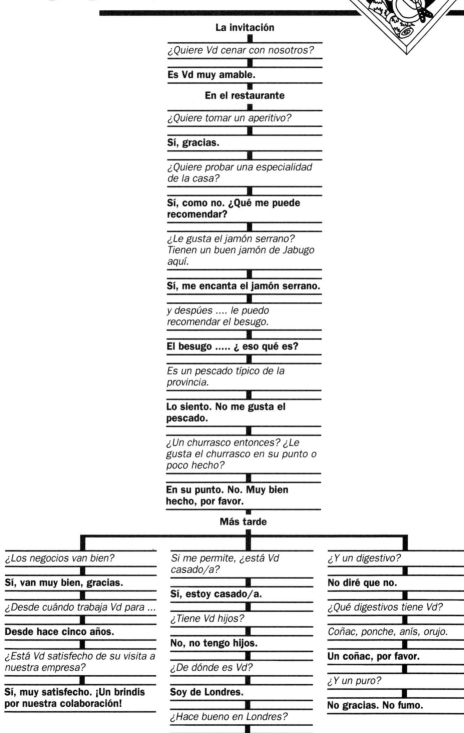

La invitación

¿Quiere Vd cenar con nosotros?

Es Vd muy amable.

En el restaurante

¿Quiere tomar un aperitivo?

Sí, gracias.

¿Quiere probar una especialidad de la casa?

Sí, como no. ¿Qué me puede recomendar?

¿Le gusta el jamón serrano? Tienen un buen jamón de Jabugo aquí.

Sí, me encanta el jamón serrano.

y despúes .... le puedo recomendar el besugo.

El besugo ..... ¿ eso qué es?

Es un pescado típico de la provincia.

Lo siento. No me gusta el pescado.

¿Un churrasco entonces? ¿Le gusta el churrasco en su punto o poco hecho?

En su punto. No. Muy bien hecho, por favor.

Más tarde

¿Los negocios van bien?

Sí, van muy bien, gracias.

¿Desde cuándo trabaja Vd para ...

Desde hace cinco años.

¿Está Vd satisfecho de su visita a nuestra empresa?

Sí, muy satisfecho. ¡Un brindis por nuestra colaboración!

Si me permite, ¿está Vd casado/a?

Sí, estoy casado/a.

¿Tiene Vd hijos?

No, no tengo hijos.

¿De dónde es Vd?

Soy de Londres.

¿Hace bueno en Londres?

No. ¡Llueve mucho!

¿Y un digestivo?

No diré que no.

¿Qué digestivos tiene Vd?

Coñac, ponche, anís, orujo.

Un coñac, por favor.

¿Y un puro?

No gracias. No fumo.

Doing business in Spain

Spanish business and social behaviour tends to be informal. Familiarity is a basic part of Spanish life. With business contacts you will very quickly get onto first name terms. However to avoid putting your foot in it, it is wise to refer to everyone as the formal **Usted** until you are invited to use the more familiar **Tú** as this will create the right framework to do business in. We have not introduced the **Tú** form in this pack for this reason.

It is quite normal at meetings, in the restaurant or in the office for men to take their jackets off or loosen their ties and 'get down to business'. It is wise to watch what your Spanish business colleagues are doing and follow suit. With the exception of grand formal occasions, manners are basically easy, relaxed and informal.

In Spain it is not the custom to offer visitors a drink on arrival, so do not feel offended if you are not offered one immediately. You'll most likely be taken to a bar for a coffee, light snack or apéritif.

Dos and Don'ts

Do shake hands when meeting someone and again when taking leave. This is a ritual that is repeated at every meeting, even amongst business colleagues who see each other every day. If there are a number of people present, go round everyone or risk being considered rude.

Do not sell yourself or your products too forcefully as the demonstration of superiority is not highly valued in Spain. Modesty is valued over assertiveness. Spanish people hold human relationships in great store and are proud of personal qualities. In fact technical ability, professionalism and competence does not concern a Spaniard as much as pride in personal qualities.

Do be punctual for meetings. The popular idea that Spaniards are laid back and believe that 'mañana will do', is not a characteristic of the small to medium sized firms you are likely to be dealing with. Most Spaniards try to cram more than is physically possible into any one day and run out of time, which is why things might be put off till 'mañana'!

Do praise Spanish 'cuisine', and be prepared to talk in some detail about food and wine. Lunches and drinks are very important in Spanish business life. During the meal, conversation will be about anything and everything under the sun until the coffee is served, whereupon the host will address the key issues. During the meal, therefore, the host will be assessing whether you could 'get on' doing business together, as the strength of a business relationship in Spain relies heavily on how well you get on personally.

Do use the Spanish you have learned on this course but, until you have become really fluent, take along an interpreter or someone who knows Spanish really well, if at all possible.

Don't try to do business in August. Business goes very quiet from mid-July to September in Spain, as people take the whole month of August off as annual leave.

What next?

Further suggestions for improving your Spanish and your knowledge of Spain.

Get some language training to supplement your private study. Even a small number of hours of tuition will boost your confidence and allow you to clarify any points that may have been troubling you. Your local college, university or polytechnic may run courses for business people or offer tutor support, on a one-to-one basis, for students using open-learning packs like **Spanish *Just for Business***. There are also many private organisations offering language training. The Association of Language Export Centres (Tel. 071 224 3748) is a useful source of information on quality providers.

Listen to the Spanish radio (for example, Radio Nacional de España which has news flashes every hour) and watch Spanish films. If you have satellite TV, the possibilities are endless!

Buy a Spanish newspaper such as *El País* or *ABC* or a weekly news magazine *Cambio 16*, once a week. Even if you only understand the headlines or the gist of the articles you will acquire useful Spanish vocabulary.

Improve your background knowledge of Spanish by reading the *Country Profile* on Spain published by the DTI. (Exports to Europe Branch, Department of Trade and Industry, 1 Victoria Street, London SW1H 0ET) or the guides published by major clearing banks. Dip into the chapter on Spain in the Industrial Society's book by John Mole *Mind Your Manners* for more information on Spanish business culture.

¡Buena suerte!

Answers to exercises

Unit 1

1 3-d, 1-b, 4-a, 2-c

2 1. Corcuera, Zaragoza   2. Solchaga, Palma de Mallorca

3 1. True 2. True 3. False 4. False

4 The only time when you are both available is this afternoon, i.e. Monday afternoon

Unit 2

1 1. Correct   2. 50-77-39   3. Correct   4. 455-28-50

3 Message 1 - c)- (ii)   Message 2 - a)- (iii)   Message 3 - b)- (iv)

4 1. The message is from Felipe López of Compresores Samur; he wants to talk to Mrs Phillips about next week's meeting.
   2. Mrs Cartwright's meeting tomorrow with Alfredo Rubiera, the head of the Export Department has been cancelled.
   3. Ana Mariá Blanco is arriving tomorrow, Tuesday, at 1.20 p.m. on flight BA254.

5 You heard the recorded messages in the order 2, 3, 1.

Unit 3

1 10.30 María Gutierrez to see Teresa Marañón and
        Isabel Pérez to see Juan García
   11.00 Rafael Giménez to see José Hernández
   11.30 Luis Velasco to see Alfonso Navarro

2 The correct order is: g, c, a, f, d, h, b, e

Unit 4

1 The order of the statements is:

A high quality product
Robust, offering a high degree of security
Modern and practical
Easy to install
Easy to clean

2 The dimensions are:
1. Small window: 80 cm diameter; large: 110cm diameter
2. Crate: 90 cm long, 70 cm wide, 50 cm high
3. Large desk: 145 cm long, 75 cm wide, 72 cm high
   Small desk: 130 cm long, 65 cm wide, 72 cm high
4. Large plate: 28 cm diameter; medium: 23 cm; small: 18cm.

Unit 5

1 **Angela Alvarez**
Founded 12 years ago; Head office in Barcelona; manufacturing plants in Spain (2), Greece and Portugal; 680 employees in total, 450 of them in Spain; turnover last year: over 12 billion pesetas; current markets: Europe and USA; future plans: to export to Japan.

Agencia de Publicidad García
Founded seven years ago; branches in Munich, Milan and London; 75 employees in Spain, 45 in other European countries; turnover last year 2.6 billion pesetas.

2 Proportion of turnover in various markets: home market 53%; rest of Europe 29%; USA 18%. Percentage increase in sales: in Spain 5%; in rest of Europe 16%; USA 30%.

3

	AX 45	AX32
In stock?	Yes	Made to order
Delivery?	15 days	6 weeks
Price?	3500 pesetas	5000 pesetas

Discounts: 2% on orders of more than 4,000,000 pesetas.
5% on orders of more than 10,000,000 pesetas.
Payment: irrevocable documentary letter of credit.

Unit 6

1 The items mentioned are:
la ensalada de mariscos
unos espárragos trigueros con mayonesa
el jamón de Jabugo
el besugo al horno
un churrasco

2 1. His son is 9 and his daughter 7
   2. His wife is a secretary. She doesn't work for Fenestral
   3. 3 years
   4. In a small village near Oxford
   5. Yes, a daughter

Language reference

Accents

In written Spanish, you will find two kinds of accents written over letters. The first ´ is found over vowels i.e. the letters 'a, e, i, o, u', (**á, é, í, ó, ú**) to indicate stress (see below). The second ~ is found over the 'n' (ñ),to indicate a different sound, such as in mañana (this new sound is similar to 'ni' in onion)

Stress
Unlike English, Spanish has clearly defined rules to help us know how to pronounce words.

1 When the word ends in a vowel e.g. **cin**co, **pue**de, or when the word ends with 'n' or 's' e.g. quisi**er**an, **tie**nen, **bue**nas **tar**des, then the stress falls on the next to last syllable.

2 When the word ends in a consonant other than 'n' or 's' e.g. co**ñac**, ta**ller**, lla**mar**, empera**dor**, the stress falls on the final syllable.

3 Otherwise an accent is written to show where the stress falls e.g. ca**fé**, mi**lí**metro, veinti**dós**, **nú**mero, avi**ón**.

Note that the use of an accent is also used to show a difference in meaning e.g.

¿Por qué? *Why?* and **Porque** ... *Because ...;*
sí *yes* and **si** *if;*
está *he/she is*, **esta** (**tarde**) *this (afternoon)* and **ésta** *this one;*
sólo *only* and **solo** *alone;*

Pronunciation guide

Spanish is much more straightforward than English in that once you have learnt a few simple rules, you can then pronounce *all* words in Spanish. In English we are never quite sure how to pronounce things until we hear someone say the word out loud because of the large number of redundant letters e.g. *Write*. In Spanish with the exception of letter *h,* all the letters are pronounced.

In this section we want to give you the rules for relating spelling to pronunciation, as we assume that you will want to use a dictionary to find words you need which do not occur in this course. For the precise pronunciation of individual sounds listen carefully to the tape and imitate it as closely as possible.

Vowels in Spanish are short and crisp. They are pronounced with the mouth wider open than in English and sound the same wherever they occur in a word.

i is similar to 'i' in machine
s**i**, **vi**no

e is similar to 'e' in **e**dible
m**e, e**sperar

a is similar to 'a' in 'that'
adiós, **a**visar

o is similar to 'o' in 'pot'
n**o**, s**o**lo

u is similar to 'oo' in 'spoon'
m**u**cho, **u**na, **U**sted

y is similar to 'i' in machine
y, mu**y**

When two vowels occur together, pronounce both.

b**ue**no ('bweno'), v**oy**

Consonants are pronounced like their English equivalents with the following exceptions:

b and **v** sound the same with lips slightly parted like a soft 'b': **b**uenos días, **b**anco, **v**ino, **v**iene

c before 'i' and 'e' and **z** before 'a', 'o' and 'u' is similar to 'th' in **th**in: **c**enar, **c**ita, pie**z**as, azú**c**ar

c before 'a' 'o' and 'u' and **qu** before 'i' and 'e' similar to 'k' in **k**itchen: **c**afé, **c**ómo, **qu**é, **qu**iero

g before 'i' and 'e' and **j** before all vowels similar to a throaty 'h': **G**imenez, embala**j**e, traba**j**ar

g before 'a' 'o' 'u' and **gu** before 'i' and 'e' similar to 'g' as in **g**arden: **g**ama, se**g**uridad, tri**gu**eros

but **gu** before 'a' is pronounced 'gw' as in a**gu**a

r in the middle of a word is slightly rolled (seño**r**a), whereas **r** at the start of a word and **rr** are strongly rolled as in Scottish 'r': **r**iñones, i**rr**evocable.

ch is similar to English 'ch' in **ch**ocolate: **ch**urrasco

ñ is similar to 'ni' in o**ni**on: ma**ñ**ana

ll is similar to 'lli' in mi**lli**on: **ll**ueve, aji**ll**o

d at the end of a word is similar to 'th' in thin:
uste**d**, Madri**d** (sometimes not pronounced at all, e.g. usté, Madrí)

h is **not** pronounced: (**h**)otel, a(**h**)ora

Numbers (los números)

0 cero

1 uno/a	11 once	21 veintiuno/a	31 treinta y uno/a
2 dos	12 doce	22 veintidós	32 treinta y dos
3 tres	13 trece	23 veintitrés	33 treinta y tres
4 cuatro	14 catorce	24 veinticuatro	34 treinta y cuatro
5 cinco	15 quince	25 veinticinco	35 treinta y cinco
6 seis	16 dieciséis	26 veintiséis	36 treinta y seís
7 siete	17 diecisiete	27 veintisiete	37 treinta y siete
8 ocho	18 dieciocho	28 veintiocho	38 treinta y ocho
9 nueve	19 diecinueve	29 veintinueve	39 treinta y nueve
10 diez	20 veinte	30 treinta	40 cuarenta

50 cincuenta
60 sesenta
70 setenta   for intermediate numbers follow
80 ochenta   the pattern 31 - 39
90 noventa

100 cien	200 doscientos/as	600 seiscientos/as
101 ciento uno/a	300 trescientos/as	700 setecientos/as
102 ciento dos	400 cuatrocientos/as	800 ochocientos/as
	500 quinientos/as	900 novecientos/as

666	seiscientos/ as sesenta y seis	2000	dos mil
1993	mil novecientos noventa y tres	1 000 000	un millón
		26 000 000 000	veintiséis billones

The time (la hora)

¿Qué hora es?	*What time is it?*
son las nueve y cinco	*9.05*
son las ocho y cuarto	*8.15*
son las once y media	*11.30*
son las siete y veinte	*7.20*
son las diez menos cuarto	*9.45*
es la una de la madrugada	*it's 1 am*
es la una del mediodía	*it's 1 pm*
son las siete de la tarde	*it's 7 pm*
¿A qué hora quedamos?	*When shall we meet?*
Quedamos a las diez y media	*Let's meet at 10.30*

The days of the week (los días de la semana)

lunes	*Monday*	ayer	*yesterday*
martes	*Tuesday*	hoy	*today*
miércoles	*Wednesday*	mañana	*tomorrow*
jueves	*Thursday*	el lunes	*on Monday*
viernes	*Friday*	el miércoles	*on Wednesday*
sábado	*Saturday*	los lunes	*on Mondays*
domingo	*Sunday*	los miércoles	*on Wednesdays*

The months of the year (los meses del año)

enero	*January*	julio	*July*
febrero	*February*	agosto	*August*
marzo	*March*	septiembre	*September*
abril	*April*	octubre	*October*
mayo	*May*	noviembre	*November*
junio	*June*	diciembre	*December*

The date (la fecha)

¿Qué es la fecha?	*What is the date?*
Es ...	*It's ...*
el uno de marzo	*1st March*
el nueve de junio	*9th June*
el veintiuno de agosto	*21st August*

Cardinal numbers are always used for dates.

¿Cuándo tiene Vd cita con Fenestral?	*When do you have an appointment with Fenestral?*
Tengo una cita el 18 de octubre	*I have an appointment on 18th October*

Note that in the above sentence 'on' is not rendered into Spanish.

Telephone numbers (Números de teléfono)

Spanish telephone numbers in large Spanish cities such as Madrid or Barcelona have 7 digits, for example 745-11-15 which would be said 7-45-11-15 or **siete - cuarenta y cinco - once - quince.**

Spanish telephone numbers **in smaller conurbations** such as Burgos, Málaga and León only have 6 digits, for example 22-04-33 which would be said **veintidós - cero, cuatro - treinta y tres.**

Verbs

Unfortunately verbs in Spanish are extremely complicated and need to be learnt by rote and by constant usage.

Detailed below are firstly two commonly occurring verbs followed by examples of regular verbs followed by a table of commonly occurring irregular verbs. We strongly recommend however for full information that you will need to refer to a dictionary or grammar book.

Ser *(to be)*		**Tener** *(to have)*	
soy	*I am*	tengo	*I have*
es	*he/she/it/Vd is*	tiene	*he/she/it/Vd has*
somos	*we are*	tenemos	*we have*
son	*they/Vds are*	tienen	*they/Vds have*

Verbs ending in

-ar	-er	-ir
hablar *(to speak)*	**comer** *(to eat)*	**vivir** *(to live)*
habl**o**	com**o**	viv**o**
habl**a**	com**e**	viv**e**
habl**amos**	com**emos**	viv**imos**
habl**an**	com**en**	viv**en**

All Spanish verbs are divided into three groups according to their ending in **-ar**, **-er**, **-ir**.

There are certain spelling changes that are applied systematically throughout the verb system to maintain the sound of the stem.

Certain regular verbs undergo a change in the vowel in the stem e.g. **contar** (to count), **cuento; perder** (to lose), **pierdo; sentir** (to feel) **siento.**

A list of common verbs

competir *(to compete)*	compito	compite	competimos	compiten
conocer *(to know a person)*	conozco	conoce	conocemos	conocen
contar *(to count, recount)*	cuento	cuenta	contamos	cuentan
decir *(to say)*	digo	dice	decimos	dicen
estar *(to be)*	estoy	está	estamos	están
hacer *(to do/make)*	hago	hace	hacemos	hacen
introducir *(to introduce)*	introduzco	introduce	introducimos	introducen
pensar *(to think)*	pienso	piensa	pensamos	piensan
perder *(to lose)*	pierdo	pierde	perdemos	pierden
poder *(to be able)*	puedo *(I can)*	puede *(he can)*	podemos *(we can)*	pueden *(they can)*
poner *(to put)*	pongo	pone	ponemos	ponen
producir *(to produce)*	produzco	produce	producimos	producen
proveer *(to supply)*	proveo	provee	proveemos	proveen
querer *(to want)*	quiero	quiere	queremos	quieren
saber *(to know a fact)*	sé	sabe	sabemos	saben
seguir *(to follow)*	sigo	sigue	seguimos	siguen
traer *(to bring)*	traigo	trae	traemos	traen
venir *(to come)*	vengo	viene	venimos	vienen
ver *(to see)*	veo	ve	vemos	ven
volver *(to return)*	vuelvo	vuelve	volvemos	vuelven

Adjectives

In Unit 4 we noted that in Spanish many adjectives follow the noun they describe. It is also important to realize that the ending changes according to the gender and number of the noun. The usual pattern is as follows:

Masculine: un jersey pequeño   *a small sweater*
                   unos jerseys pequeños   *small sweaters*

Feminine: una ventana pequeña   *a small window*
                   unas ventanas pequeñas   *small windows*

Don't let fear of making mistakes in this inhibit you from speaking Spanish! In most cases you will still be understood even if you forget to make the adjectives and noun agree. However it'll ease communication if you learn the masculine and feminine forms of at least a few of the commonly occurring adjectives.

Vocabulary

Notes

1 The gender of nouns is indicated by the article (**el** or **los** - masculine, and **la** or **las** - feminine).
2 Feminine forms of adjectives are separated by an oblique: **alto/a.**
3 Both the infinitive and the first person singular are given for Spanish irregular verbs. Only the infinitive is given for regular verbs.

Abbreviations

f. = feminine
m. = masculine
sing. = singular
pl. = plural
adv. = adverb
tel. = for use on telephone

Spanish - English

A

a to
¿A qué hora (tiene Vd la reunión)? What time (is your meeting)?
abrir to open
acabado: se ha acabado... we have no more...
adelantar to bring forward
adiós goodbye
la **agencia de publicidad** advertising agency
la **agenda** diary
el **agua mineral con gas/sin gas** fizzy/still mineral water
ahora now
ahora le paso/pongo I'm putting you through
la **Alemania** Germany
alergia: tener alergia to be allergic
algo something
alguien someone

el **almacén** storage area
el **aluminio** aluminium
alto/a high
  de alto high; tall (adv.)
amable kind
ancho/a wide
  de ancho wide (adv.)
antes before
antes de las once before 11 am
el **año** year
  el año anterior last year
el **aperitivo** apéritif
  de apertura al exterior opening outwards
aplazar to postpone
apreciar to appreciate
aproximadamente approximately
aquí here
aquí está... here you have...
aquí tiene... here is...
los **artículos de cuero** leather goods
la **asistencia posventa** after-sales service

aumentar to increase
aumentado increased
el **aumento** increase
las **aves y (la) caza** poultry and game
ayudar to help

B

barril: de barril draught (beer)
bastante quite
el **besugo al horno** sea bream baked in
  the oven
bien O.K.; good
blanco/a white
bonito/a pretty
el **bonito con tomate** tuna braised in
  tomato
la **botella** bottle
el **botellín** bottle of beer (1/5 litre)
el **brindis** toast (*raise your glasses to...*)
buenas noches good night (*only said as*
  you go off to bed!)
buenas tardes good afternoon/evening
  (*any time after 4 pm*)
buenos días good morning (*until 2 pm*)
buscar to go and get; to find

C

el **café** coffee
un café solo a black coffee
un café con leche y azúcar a coffee
  with milk and sugar
un café con leche en taza grande a
  large milky coffee.
un cortado a coffee with very little milk
la **calidad** quality
  de alta calidad high quality
el **calor** heat
  hace calor it's hot weather
  tengo calor I'm hot
cada each
la **calle de dirección única** one way
  street
cambiar to change
cancelar cancel
la **caravana (de 8 kilómetros)** (5 mile)
  tail-back
la **carne** meat
la **carta** menu; letter
el **cartón** cardboard
estar casado/a to be married
cenar to have dinner

la **centralita** switch board operator; telephonist
cerrar (cierro) to close (I close)
la **cerveza** beer
la **cerveza de barril** draught beer
los **champiñones rellenos** stuffed mushrooms
el **chico** boy
la **chica** girl
Chin, chin! Cheers!
los **chipirones rebozados** baby squid in
  batter
el **churrasco de ternera** T-bone steak
cien a hundred
cinco five
cinco por ciento 5%
la **cita** appointment
la **ciudad** city
el **cliente** client
el **coche** car
la **cocina española** Spanish cooking
el **cochinillo asado** roast sucking pig
las **codornices estofadas** braised quail
el **color** colour
comer to have lunch; to eat
la **comida** lunch
  ¡una comida muy prolongada! an
  endless lunch!
  una comida de negocios a business
  lunch
¿cómo...? how...?; what did you say?
¿cómo está Vd? how are you?
¿cómo se escribe...? how do you spell...?
¿cómo se llama su empresa/compañía?
  what is the name of your company?
como siempre as usual
la **compañía** company
la **competencia** competition
comprar to buy
comprobar (compruebo) to check
  (I check)
lo **comprobaré en la oficina** I'll check with
  the office
lo **hemos comprobado** we've checked
comunicando: está comunicando the
  line's engaged
con with
el **concesionario** agent
las **condiciones de pago** payment terms
concertar una cita con to make an
  appointment with
el **conejo al ajillo** braised rabbit with garlic
confirmar to confirm
el **contrato** contract
contra factura against invoice

el **coñac** brandy
conocer (conozco) to know s.o. (I know s.o.)
convenir to suit
el **cordero asado** roast lamb
el **correo** post
por correo certificado by registered post
el **crecimiento** growth
el **crédito documentario irrevocable** irrevocable letter of credit
el **cristal** glass
la **cuajada** a kind of set yoghurt
¿cuál(es)...? which...?; what...?
¿cuál es el precio de...? what is the price of...?
¿cuándo...? when...?
¿cuánto...? how much...?
¿cuánto es? how much is it?
¿cuántos(as)...? how many...?
cuatro four
a las cuatro at (exactly) four o'clock
sobre las cuatro around four o'clock
la **cuenta** bill
cumplir to conform (to a standard)

D

dar un precio to give a price
del/de la/de los/de las of the
de acuerdo O.K.!
de alto high; tall (adv.)
de ancho wide (adv.)
de barril draught (beer)
de espesor thick (adv.)
de largo long (adv.)
de nada think nothing of it
de vacaciones on holiday
de (uPVC) made of (uPVC)
decir (digo) to say (I say)
¿de dónde es Vd? where are you from?
deletrear to spell
dejar un mensaje to leave a message
dentro de quince minutos in 15 minutes
dentro de poco in a little while
el **departamento** the department
el **departamento de compras** purchasing department
el **departamento de contabilidad** accounts department
el **departamento de exportación** export department
el **departamento de importación** import department

el **departamento de marketing** marketing department
el **departamento de personal** personnel department
el **departamento de producción** production department
el **departamento técnico** technical department
el **departamento de ventas** sales department
¡depende! it depends!
la **dependienta** sales assistant
derecha: a la derecha on the right
el **descafeinado** decaffeinated coffee
¿desde cuándo hace Vd eso? how long have you done this?
desde hace mucho tiempo for ages; for a long time
mi despacho my office
despúes after(wards)
el **diámetro** diameter
de diámetro in diameter (adv.)
diez ten
¡dígame! tell me!
el **digestivo** liqueur
la **dimensión** dimension
la **dirección** address
de dirección única one way (street)
el **director/la directora del departament de exportación** export director
el **director general** managing director
el **diseño** design
dos two
a las doce (de mediodía) at midday
el **dueño** owner

E

elegir (elijo) to choose (I choose)
el **embalaje** crate; packaging
el **embotellamiento** traffic jam
el **emperador a la plancha** grilled swordfish
el **empleado** employee
empezar (empiezo) to start (I start)
la **empresa** company
una empresa mediana a medium-sized company
en in
en el extranjero abroad
en invierno in winter
en reunión in a meeting
en seguida straightaway
en viaje de negocios away on business
me encantan (las patatas fritas) I love (chips)

encantado/a pleased to meet you; hello
encontrar (encuentro) to find (I find)
enfermo/a ill
la **ensalada de marisco** mixed seafood salad
una **ensalada mixta** mixed salad of tomato and lettuce
enseñarle algo a alguién to show someone something
entender (entiendo) to understand (I understand)
no le entiendo bien I don't understand (you)
entonces then
la **entrada** first course
el **entrecote de buey** rib of beef
la **entrega** delivery
enviar to send by post
el **envío** sending by post
es you (sing.) are; he/she is
esa; esas (f.) that; those
es cierto it's true!; that's true
escribir to write
escocés/esa Scottish
es decir that is; in other words
eso; esos (m.) that; those
eso es that's right
¿eso qué es? what's that?
especial special
la **especialidad de la casa** speciality of the restaurant
esperar to wait for
está he/she is
esta mesa this table
esta tarde this afternoon
los **Estados Unidos (los EE.UU.)** the United States
estar bien to be O.K.
estar especializado(s) en to specialize in
esto; estos this; these
los **espárragos trigueros con mayonesa** asparagus with mayonnaise
este año this year
estoy casado/a I'm married
en el estranjero abroad
europeo/a European
exactamente that's right
el **éxito** success
la **extensión** extensión
exportar to export

F

fabricar (fabricamos) to make (we make)
fácilmente easily
la **factura** invoice
la **familia** family
familiar family (adj.)*as in* family business
el **Faria** typical Spanish cigar
la **fecha** date
los **fiambres** cold meats
el **fino** dry sherry
el **flan** caramel custard
el **folleto** brochure
Francia France
la **fresa** strawberry
frío/a cold
tengo frío I'm cold
hace frío it's cold weather
la **fruta** fruit
fuera away
fuerte strong
fumar to smoke
fundar to establish (a company)

G

la **gama** range
una **gama de productos** product range
una **gama amplia de productos** large product range
las **gambas al ajillo** garlic prawns
garantizado/a guaranteed
gracias thanks
gracias, no no thanks
grande large; big; great
gustar (me gusta/an) to please (I like)
no me gusta/an I don't like
el **gusto** pleasure
¡el gusto ha sido mío! the pleasure was mine!

H

hablar to speak
al **habla** (tel.) speaking; on the line
¿habla Vd inglés? do you speak English?
hacer (hago) to do; make (I do; make)
hace bueno/calor/frío it's fine/hot/cold
hace ago
hace cuarenta años 40 years ago
hacer un pedido to place an order
¡hasta luego! see you later!

¡**hasta pronto!** see you (very) soon!
hay there is/are
hay un descuento de 5% there's a
  discount of 5%
hecho(s) a mano hand-made
el **helado** ice-cream
el **hielo** ice
la **hierba** herb
la **hija** daughter
hola hello
la **Holanda** Holland
holandés/a Dutch
hoy today
la **huelga** strike

I

el **ingeniero** engineer
inglés/a English
instalar to install
interesante interesting
internacional international
introducirse to enter (a market)
interior internal (adj.)
el **mercado interior** the home market
la **invitación** invitation
el **invierno** winter
ir a (voy a) to go to (I go/am going to)
izquierda: a la izquierda on the left

J

el **jamón de Jabugo** Jabugo (dry cured)
  ham
el **Japón** Japan
¡**Jefe!** Waiter!
el **jefe del departamento** head of the
  department
el **jersey** pullover
jóven young
el **jueves** (on) Thursday

L

el **lanzamiento de un nuevo producto**
  new product launch
largo/a long
de **largo** long (adv.)
las the *for plural feminine words e.g.* las
  ventanas - the windows
libre free
estoy libre el miércoles o el jueves I'm

free on Wednesday or Thursday
ligero/a lightweight
el **limón** lemon
limpiar to clean
la **lista de precios** price list
listo/a ready
llamar to ring/call back
llegar to arrive
llueve it's raining
lo siento I'm sorry; I apologize
los the *for plural masculine words e.g.* los
  jerseys - the pullovers
el **lunes** (on) Monday
el **lunes que viene** next Monday

M

la **madre** mother
la **madera** wood
de madera made of wood
el **maletín** briefcase
la **manilla** handle
mañana por la mañana tomorrow
  morning
mañana por la tarde tomorrow afternoon
el **marisco** seafood
el **martes** Tuesday
más de more than
más o menos more or less
más tarde later
más tarde, esta mañana later, this
  morning
mayor older
me informaré I'll find out
mediano/a medium-sized
medio pollo asado half a roast chicken
mejor que better than
la **menestra de verduras** mixed vegetable
  stew
menos de less than
el **menú del día** set menu
el **mercado (interior)** the (home) market
el **mes** month
un **mes y medio** a month and a half
mi my
mi mujer my wife
el **miércoles** Wednesday
mismo/a same
el **modelo** style
moderno/a modern
molestar to disturb
el **momento** moment
mucho a lot; many

mucho gusto pleased to meet you; hello
muchas gracias thank you very much
muchas gracias por su visita thank you for your visit
una **muestra** sample
la **mujer** woman
muy very
muy bien very well
muy bien hecho very well done (steak)

N

nada nothing
de **nada** think nothing of it
la **naranja** orange
el **néctar de melocotón** peach drink (*mixture of juice and water*)
los **negocios** business
negro/a black
ni...ni... neither...nor...
nieva it's snowing
la **noche** night
    esta **noche** this evening; tonight
las **normas europeas** European standards
el **nombre** name
el **nombre de pila** first name
el **nombre de mi empresa es...** the name of my company is...
no no *or* not
no cuelgue, por favor (tel.) hold on, please
¡No diré que no! I won't say no!
¡No me extraña! I'm not surprised!; I might have guessed!
no estoy casado/a I'm not married
no hay de qué It's not important; don't mention it!
no hay mucha competencia we haven't got much competition
no importa it doesn't matter
no importa, no tiene importancia don't worry, it's alright
no me gusta I don't like
no lo sé I don't know
no sé exactamente I'm not quite sure
no se preocupe don't worry; it's alright
no tengo hijos I have no children
no, de ninguna manera no, not at all
no, para mí, no. Gracias not for me.
nuestro/a our
nueve nine
nuevo/a new
el **número** number

el **número de teléfono es...** the telephone number is...

O

ocho eight
ocupado/a busy
la **oficina** office
original unusual; original
otro/a other

P

el **país** country
la **parte** part; behalf
¿de parte de quién, por favor? (tel.) who's calling, please?
pasado mañana the day after tomorrow
el **pastel** cake
las **patatas fritas** chips
el **pedido** the order
pequeño/a small
perdone Sorry!; Excuse me!
perdonar to excuse
perdone... excuse me ...
perdone, creo que hay una pequeña confusión excuse me, I think there's been a slight misunderstanding
permitir to allow
el **pescado** fish
las **piezas de recambio/piezas de repuesto** spare parts
una **pieza suelta** one single part
los **pimientos a la riojana** sweet peppers stuffed with minced lamb
la **piña** pineapple
el **pisto** ratatouille
el **plato** dish
el **plato principal** main course
el **plazo de entrega** delivery time
poco: un poco más for a while; a bit longer
poder: (puedo) to be able (I can)
puede llamarle... (tel.) you can call back
el **porcentaje** percentage
el **porcentaje exacto es de 25%** the exact percentage is 25%
por año per year
por ejemplo for example
por favor please
por la tarde in the afternoon
por mes per month
por semana per week

posible possible
el **postre** dessert
práctico/a practical
el **precio** price
unos **precios muy competitivos** very competitive prices
preferir (prefiero) to prefer (I prefer)
el **prefijo es...** (tel.) the code is...
la **pregunta** question
presentar to introduce
le **presento a...** let me introduce...
primero/a first
probar (pruebo) to try (I try)
el **producto** product
los **productos de belleza** beauty products
prolongado/a endless
promedio: de promedio on average
el **proveedor** supplier
provincia: en la provincia locally
el **pueblo** town
pues well
punto: en su punto medium (*for a steak*)
el **puro** cigar

Q

¡Que aproveche! Have a good meal!
querer (quiero) to want (I want)
querido/a dear
el **queso** cheese
quien who
¿quiere...? would you like...?
quisiera... I'd like to...
quizás perhaps

R

rápido/a rapid
razón: tener razón to be right
la **recepcionista** receptionist
recomendar to recommend
el **refresco** soft drink
regular (it was) not too bad
la **relación** relation(ship)
con **relación al año anterior** compared to last year
repetir to repeat
el **restaurante** restaurant
resistente hard-wearing
el **retraso** delay
reunido/a in a meeting
la **reunión** meeting

rico/a tasty
los **riñones al jerez** kidneys braised in sherry

S

saber to know (a fact)
no Bosé I don't know
el **sabor** flavour
satisfecho/a: estar satisfecho de to be satisfied with
seco/a dry
la **secretaria** secretary
la **sede social** company headquarters
seis six
seguir (sigo) to follow (I follow)
en **seguida** straightaway
la **semana** week
esta **semana** this week
la **semana que viene** next week
el **señor** gentleman
la **señora** lady
la **señorita** young lady
sentarse (me siento) to sit down (I sit)
el **septiembre** September
ser to be
ser experto en to be an expert in
será it/you/he/she will be
serie: de serie standard
el **servicio** service
el **servicio de asistencia posventa** after-sales service department
si if
si me permite... if I may be so bold ...
sí yes
sí, como no I wouldn't mind!
sí, gracias yes, please
sí, perfectamente yes, easily ; no problem
sí, por supuesto yes, of course!
siempre always
lo **siento...** I'm sorry ...
siete seven
sin without
sin gas still (*as in mineral water*)
sin embargo however
sobre pedido made to order
el **socio** business colleague
solamente only
somos we are
son you are (pl.); they are
la **sopa castellana** country garlic soup
la **sopa de pescado** fish soup
soy I am
soy.... my name is ....

soy de Sheffield/Glasgow I'm from Sheffield/Glasgow
stock: en stock in stock
suficientemente enough (adv.)
sugerir (sugiero) to suggest (I suggest)
su your/his/her
suponer (supongo) to suppose (I suppose)
su nombre your name
la **sucursal** branch
superar to exceed

T

también also
la **tarta helada** frozen cream-cake with ice-cream
el **té** tea
tener (tengo) to have (I have/have got)
tener 5 años to be 5 years old
tener en proyecto to intend to; to plan to
tener razón to be right
tener una cita con... to have an appointment with...
el **tiempo** weather
típico/a typical
el **tipo de clientela** client type
todo el tiempo all the time
todavía still; yet
tomar to have (a drink)
trabajar to work
el **trabajo** work; job
tradicional traditional
el **tráfico** traffic
traer (traigo) to bring (I bring)
tráiganos... bring us...
trata: ¿De qué se trata? What is it about?
tres three
el **turrón** almond and honey sweetmeat

U

uno/a one
la **unidad** unit

x **unidades de producción** x production units
uPVC uPVC
urgentemente urgently
utilizar to use

V

vainilla vanilla
vamos a pasar a mi despacho let's go through to my office
varios/as several
Vd/s (usted/ustedes) you *polite sing. & pl. forms*
veamos let's see
ver to see
verdaderamente truly
veinte twenty
vender to sell
las **ventas** sales
la **ventana** window
verano: en verano in summer
¿verdad? don't you?; isn't that right?
viajar (mucho) to travel (a lot)
el **viaje** journey
el **viernes** (on) Friday
el **vino** wine
un **vino blanco** a (glass of) white wine
un **vino tinto** a (glass of) red wine
vino(s) del país local wine(s)
visitar to visit
la **visita** visit
vivir (en Londres) to live (in London)
vivo/a bright (colour)
el **volumen de ventas** turnover
volver (vuelvo) to go back (I go back)

Y

y and

Z

la **zona de embalaje** packing area
el **zumo (de naranja)** (orange) juice

Vocabulary

English - Spanish

A

abroad en el extranjero
accounts department el departamento de contabilidad
address la dirección
advertising agency la agencia de publicidad
after-sales service la asistencia posventa
after-sales service department el servicio de asistencia posventa
after(wards) después
against invoice contra factura
agent el concesionario
ago hace
ages: for ages desde hace mucho tiempo
almond and honey sweetmeat el turrón
also también
aluminium el aluminio
allergic: to be allergic tener alergia
all the time todo el tiempo
to **allow** permitir
always siempre
and y
apéritif un aperitivo
appointment la cita
to **appreciate** apreciar
approximately aproximadamente
around four o'clock sobre las cuatro
to **arrive** llegar
asparagus with mayonnaise (los) espárragos trigueros con mayonesa
as usual como siempre
at four o'clock (precisely) a las cuatro
away fuera
away on business en viaje de negocios
average: on average de promedio

B

baby squid in batter (los) chipirones rebozados
to **be** ser
be: it/you/he/she will be será
to **be able (I can)** poder (puedo)
to **be an expert in** ser experto en
to **be 5 years old** tener 5 años
beauty products (los) productos de belleza
beer una cerveza
before antes
before 11 am antes de las once
better than mejor que
bill la cuenta
black negro/a
black coffee un café solo
bottle la botella
a bottle of beer (1/5 litre) un botellín
boy el chico
braised quail (las) codornices estofadas
braised rabbit with garlic (el) conejo al ajillo
branch sucursal
brandy un coñac
briefcase el maletín
bright (colour) vivo/a
to **bring (I bring)** traer (traigo)
to **bring forward** adelantar
bring us... tráiganos...
brochure el folleto
business los negocios
a business lunch una comida de negocios
busy ocupado/a
to **buy** comprar
by registered post por correo certificado

C

cake el pastel
frozen cream-cake with ice-cream la tarta helada
to **cancel** cancelar
car el coche
caramel custard el flan
cardboard el cartón
to **change** cambiar
to **check (I check)** comprobar (compruebo)
Cheers! ¡Chin, chin!
cheese el queso
chips las patatas fritas
to **choose (I choose)** elegir (elijo)
cigar el puro
city la ciudad
to **clean** limpiar
client el cliente
client type el tipo de clientela
to **close (I close)** cerrar (cierro)
code: the (telephone) code is... el prefijo es...
coffee el café
a coffee with milk and sugar un café con leche y azúcar
a coffee with very little milk un cortado
cold frío/a
cold drink el refresco
colleague: business colleague el socio
colour el color
company la compañía/empresa
company headquarters la sede social
compared to last year con relación al año anterior
competition la competencia
to **confirm**
to **conform (to a standard)** cumplir
contract el contrato
country el país
country garlic soup la sopa castellana
crate unembalaje

D

date la fecha
daughter la hija
day after tomorrow pasado mañana
dear querido/a
decaffeinated coffee el descafeinado
delay el retraso
delivery la entrega
delivery time el plazo de entrega

department el departamento
depend: it depends! ¡depende!
desk una mesa de trabajo
design el diseño
dessert el postre
diary la agenda
dimension la dimensión
to **have dinner** cenar
dish el plato
to **disturb** molestar
do you speak English? ¿habla Vd inglés?
to **do/make (I do/make)** hacer (hago)
don't mention it! no hay de qué
don't worry, it's alright: it's not important no importa, no tiene importancia
don't you? ¿verdad?
draught beer la cerveza de barril
drink: a (cold) drink un refresco
dry seco/a
Dutch holandés/a

E

each cada
easily fácilmente
eight ocho
employee el empleado
endless prolongado/a
engineer el ingeniero
English inglés/a
enough (adv.) suficientemente
to **enter (a market)** introducirse
to **establish (a company)** fundar
European europeo/a
European standards las normas europeas
exact percentage is 25% el porcentaje exacto es 25%
to **exceed** superar
to **excuse** perdonar
excuse me... perdone ...
extensión la extensión
to **export** exportar
export department el departamento de exportación
export director el director/la directora del departamento de exportación

F

family la familia
family (adj.) *as in* **family business** familiar

to **find (I find)** encontrar (encuentro)

finished: we have no more... (se ha) acabado...

first primero/a

first course la entrada

fish el pescado

fish soup la sopa de pescado

five cinco

five per cent cinco por ciento

fizzy (mineral water) (un agua mineral) con gas

flavour el sabor

to **follow (I follow)** seguir (sigo)

for a while; a bit longer un poco; un poco más

for ages desde hace mucho tiempo

for example por ejemplo

forty years ago hace cuarenta años

four cuatro

France la Francia

Friday el viernes

fruit la fruta

G

garlic prawns las gambas al ajillo

gentleman el señor

Germany la Alemania

girl la chica

to **give a price** dar un precio

glass (material) el cristal

to **go** ir

I am going to... voy a...

to **go and get; to find** buscar

to **go back/return (I go back/return)** volver (vuelvo)

good bien (adv.); bueno/a (adj.)

good afternoon: evening *(any time after 4 pm)* buenas tardes

good morning *(until 2 pm)* buenos días

good night *(said on going to bed)* buenas noches

goodbye adiós

grilled swordfish el emperador a la plancha

growth el crecimiento

guaranteed garantizado/a

H

half a roast chicken medio pollo asado

hand-made hecho(s) a mano

handle; window handle la manilla

Have a good meal! ¡Que aproveche!

hard-wearing resistente

to **have (I have/have got)** tener (tengo)

to **have a drink** tomar (una bebida)

to **have an appointment with** tener una cita con

he/she is está

head of the department el jefe del departamento

hello hola

to **help** ayudar

herb la hierba

here aquí

here is my card aquí tiene mi tarjeta

here you have the production line aquí está la cadena de producción

high alto/a

high; tall (adv.) de alto

high quality de alta calidad

hold on, please no cuelgue, por favor

Holland la Holanda

home (market) (el mercado) interior

hot: I am hot tengo calor

how...? ¿cómo ...?

how are you? ¿cómo está Vd?

how do you spell that? ¿cómo se escribe?

however sin embargo

how long (have you done this?) ¿desde cuándo (hace Vd eso?)

how many ...? ¿cuántos /as ...?

how much ...? ¿cuánto ...?

how much is it? ¿cuánto es?

hundred cien

I

I am soy; estoy

ice el hielo

ice-cream el helado

I'd like to... quisiera ...

I don't like... no me gusta/an ...

I have no children no tengo hijos

I'll check with the office lo comprobaré en la oficina

I'll find out me informaré

I love (chips) me encantan (las patatas fritas)

I'm cold tengo frío

I'm free on Wednesday or Thursday (estoy) libre el miércoles o el jueves

I'm from Sheffield/Glasgow soy de Sheffield/Glasgow

I'm hot tengo calor

I'm married estoy casado/a

I'm not married no estoy casado/a
I'm not quite sure no sé exactamente
I'm not surprised!: I might have guessed ¡No me extraña!
I'm putting you through ahora le paso/pongo
I'm sorry; I apologize lo siento
I won't say no! ¡No diré que no!
I wouldn't mind sí, como no
if si
if I may be so bold si me permite
ill enfermo/a
import department el departamento de importación
in en
in 15 minutes dentro de quince minutos
in a little while dentro de poco
in a meeting en reunión
in a meeting reunido/a
in diameter (adv.) de diámetro
in summer en verano
in stock en stock
in the afternoon por la tarde
in winter en invierno
to **increase** aumentar
increased aumentado
increase: an increase un aumento
to **install** instalar
to **intend to; to plan to** tener en proyecto
interesting interesante
international internacional
to **introduce** presentar
invitation la invitación
invoice la factura
isn't that right? ¿verdad?
it doesn't matter no importa
it's alright: don't worry no se preocupe
it's cold weather hace frío
it's fine/hot/cold hace bueno/calor/frío
it's hot weather hace calor
it's not important no hay de qué
it's true!; that's true es cierto

J

Japan el Japón
job el trabajo
journey el viaje

K

kidneys braised in sherry (los) riñones al jerez
kind amable
to **know: I know (s.o.)** conocer/conozco
to **know (a fact)** saber
I don't know no lo sé

L

lady la señora
large; big grande
a large discount un descuento grande
large milky coffee el café con leche en taza grande
last year al año anterior
later más tarde
later this morning más tarde esta mañana
leather goods artículos de cuero
to **leave a message** dejar un mensaje
left: on the left a la izquierda
lemon el limón
less than menos de
let me introduce... le presento a ...
let's go through to my office vamos a pasar a mi despacho
letter la carta
lightweight ligero/a
line's engaged (está) comunicando
liqueur el digestivo
to **live (I live in London)** vivir (vivo en Londres)
locally en la provincia
long largo/a
long (adv.) de largo
for a long time desde hace mucho tiempo
a lot; many mucho(s)
lunch la comida
an endless lunch! ¡una comida muy prolongada!
to **have lunch; to eat** comer

M

made of (uPVC) de (uPVC)
made by hand a mano
maincourse el plato principal
to **make (we make)** fabricar (fabricamos)
to **make an appointment with** tener una cita con

make: make to order fabricar sobre pedido
managing director el director/la directora general
market: home market el mercado interior
marketing department el departamento de marketing
married: to be married estar casado/a
to **measure** medir (mido)
meat la carne
medium (steak) en su punto
medium-sized mediano/a
a medium-sized company una empresa mediana
meeting la reunión
menu la carta
menu: the set menu el menú del día
mention: don't mention it! no hay de qué
midday a las doce (de mediodía)
mixed salad of tomato and lettuce la ensalada mixta
mixed seafood salad la ensalada de marisco
mixed vegetable stew la menestra de verduras
modern moderno/a
moment el momento
Monday el lunes
month el mes
a month and a half un mes y medio
more: (we have no) more... (se ha) acabado...
more or less más o menos
more than más de
mother la madre
my mi
my name is... soy...

N

name el nombre
first name el nombre de pila
the name of my company is... el nombre de mi empresa es ...
neither... nor... ni... ni...
new nuevo/a
new product launch el lanzamiento de un nuevo producto
next Monday el lunes que viene
next week la semana que viene
nine nueve
night la noche
no; not no

no, not at all no, de ninguna manera
no thanks gracias, no
not bad: (it was) not too bad regular
not for me no, para mí, no. Gracias
now ahora
number el número

O

of the del/de la/de los/de las
office el despacho; la oficina
OK! de acuerdo
older mayor
on holiday de vacaciones
on the left a la izquierda
on the right a la derecha
one uno/a
one way street la calle de dirección única
only solamente
to **open** abrir
opening outwards de apertura al exterior
orange la naranja
original original
other otro/a/os/as
our nuestro/a/os/as
owner el dueño

P

packaging el embalaje
packing area la zona de embalaje
part: behalf la parte
payment terms las condiciones de pago
peach el melocotón
per month por mes
per week por semana
per year por año
percentage el porcentaje
perhaps quizás
personnel department el departamento de personal
pineapple la piña
to **place an order** hacer un pedido
please por favor
to **please (I like)** gustar (me gusta/an)
pleased to meet you; hello mucho gusto; encantado/a
pleasure el gusto
pleasure was mine! ¡el gusto ha sido mío!
possible posible
post el correo
to **post** enviar
sending by post el envío

to postpone aplazar
poultry and game (las) aves y (la) caza
practical práctico/a
to prefer (I prefer) preferir (prefiero)
pretty bonito/a
price el precio
price list la lista de precios
product el producto
product range la gama de productos
production department el departamento de producción
pullover el jersey
purchasing department el departamento de compras

Q

quality la calidad
question la pregunta
quite bastante

R

rain: it's raining llueve
range la gama
rapid rápido/a
ratatouille el pisto
ready listo/a
receptionist la recepcionista
to recommend recomendar
red wine el vino tinto
relation(ship) la relación
to repeat repetir
respectable serio
restaurant el restaurante
rib of beef el entrecote de buey
right: to be right tener razón
on the right a la derecha
to ring back llamar
roast lamb el cordero asado
roast sucking pig el cochinillo asado
round redondo/a

S

sales las ventas
sales assistant la dependienta
sales department el departamento de ventas
same: the same el mismo; la misma
sample muestra; modelo
satisfied with satisfecho/a de

to (I say) decir (digo)
sea bream baked in the oven el besugo al horno
seafood el marisco
secretary la secretaria
to see ver
let's see veamos
see you later! ¡hasta luego!
see you (very) soon! ¡hasta pronto!
to sell vender
September el septiembre
service el servicio
seven siete
several varios/as
sherry: a dry sherry un fino
to show someone something enseñarle algo a alguién
single: one single part una pieza suelta
to sit down (I sit) sentarse (me siento)
six *seis*
small pequeño/a
to smoke fumar
snow: it's snowing nieva
someone alguien
something algo
sorry! ¡perdone!
spare parts las piezas de recambio; piezas de repuesto
Spanish cooking la cocina española
to speak hablar
speaking: on the line (tel.) al habla
special especial
speciality of the restaurant la especialidad de la casa
to specialize in estar especializado(s) en
to spell deletrear
standard de serie
to start (I start) empezar (empiezo)
States (U.S.A.) los Estados Unidos (los EE.UU.)
still todavía
still *(as in mineral water)* sin gas
storage area el almacén
straightaway en seguida
strike la huelga
strong fuerte
stuffed mushrooms (los) champiñones rellenos
strawberry la fresa
success el éxito
to suggest (I suggest) sugerir (sugiero)
to suit convenir
summer el verano
supplier el proveedor
to suppose (I suppose) suponer (supongo)

sweet peppers stuffed with minced lamb los pimientos a la riojana
switch board operator; telephonist la centralita

T

T-bone steak el churrasco de ternera
tasty rico/a
tea el té
technical department el departamento técnico
telephone number el número de teléfono
telephonist: switch board operator la centralita
tell me dígame
ten diez
terms; payment terms las condiciones de pago
thanks gracias
thank you for your visit muchas gracias por su visita
thank you very much muchas gracias
that/those eso/esos
that table esa mesa
these models estos modelos
those models esos modelos
that is; in other words es decir
that's right eso es
that's right exactamente
then entonces
there is/are hay
there's a discount of 5% hay un descuento de 5%
thick (adv.) de espesor
think nothing of it de nada
this/these esto/estos
this table esta mesa
this afternoon esta tarde
this evening esta noche
this week esta semana
this year este año
three tres
Thursday el jueves
toast (raise your glasses to ...) un brindis
today hoy
tomorrow afternoon mañana, por la tarde
tomorrow morning mañana por la mañana
tonight esta noche
town el pueblo

traditional tradicional
traffic jam el embotellamiento
traffic el tráfico
travel: I travel a lot viajo mucho
truly verdaderamente
to **try (I try)** probar (pruebo)
Tuesday el martes
tuna braised in tomato el bonito con tomate
turnover el volumen de ventas
twenty veinte
twenty per cent veinte por ciento
two dos
typical típico/a

U

to **understand (I understand)** entender (entiendo)
unit la unidad
unusual original
urgently urgentemente
to **use** utilizar

V

vanilla vainilla
very muy
very competitive prices unos precios muy competitivos
very well muy bien
to **visit** visitar
visit la visita

W

to **wait for** esperar
Waiter! ¡Jefe!
to **want (I want)** querer (quiero)
we are somos
we've checked lo hemos comprobado
we haven't got much competition no hay mucha competencia
we specialize in estamos especializados en
weather el tiempo
Wednesday el miércoles
week la semana
well... pues...
well: very well done (steak) muy bien hecho
what did you say? ¿cómo?

What time (is your meeting)? ¿A qué hora (tiene Vd la reunión)?

what is it about? ¿de qué se trata?

what is the name of your company? ¿cómo se llama su empresa/compañía?

what is the price of ...? ¿cuál es el precio de ...?

what's that? ¿eso qué es?

when? ¿cuándo?

where are you from? ¿De dónde es Vd?

which...? or what...? ¿cuál(es) ...?

white blanco/a

who? quién?

Who's calling, please? ¿de parte de quién, por favor?

wide ancho/a

wide (adv.) de ancho

will: it/you/he/she will be será

window la ventana

wine el vino

   a red wine un vino tinto

   a white wine un vino blanco

   local wine(s) vino(s) del país

winter el invierno

with con

without sin

woman la mujer

wood: (made of) wood (de) madera

would you like...? ¿quiere ...?

to **work** trabajar

work el trabajo

to **write** escribir

Y

year el año

yes sí

yes, easily; no problem sí, perfectamente

yes, of course! sí, por supuesto

yes, please sí, gracias

yet todavía

you (sing.) usted (*written* Vd)

you are (sing.); he/she is es

you (pl.) ustedes (written Vds)

you are (pl.); they are son; estan

you can call back puede llamar

young jóven

young lady la señorita

your su

your name su nombre